PEN

THE BIRTH OF TRAGEDY

FRIEDRICH NIETZSCHE was born near Leipzig in 1844, the son of a Lutheran clergyman. He attended the famous Pforta School, then went to university at Bonn and at Leipzig, where he studied philology and read Schopenhauer. When he was only twenty-four he was appointed to the chair of classical philology at Basle University; he stayed there until his health forced him into retirement in 1879. While at Basle he made and broke his friendship with Wagner, participated as an ambulance orderly in the Franco-Prussian War, and published *The Birth of Tragedy* (1872), *Untimely Meditations* (1873–6) and the first part of *Human, All Too Human* (1878; two supplements entitled *Assorted Opinions and Maxims* and *The Wanderer and his Shadow* followed in 1879 and 1880 respectively). From 1880 until his final collapse in 1889, except for brief interludes, he divorced himself from everyday life and, supported by his university pension, he lived mainly in France, Italy and Switzerland. *The Dawn* appeared in 1881 followed by *The Gay Science* in the autumn of 1882. *Thus Spoke Zarathustra* was written between 1883 and 1885, and his last completed books were *Ecce Homo*, an autobiography, and *Nietzsche contra Wagner*. He became insane in 1889 and remained in a condition of mental and physical paralysis until his death in 1900.

SHAUN WHITESIDE was was born in Dungannon, Northern Ireland, in 1959, and educated at Dungannon Royal School and King's College, Cambridge, where he graduated with a First in Modern Languages. He has translated widely from German, French and Italian, and his translations of Arthur Schnitzler's *Beatrice and Her Son* and Robert Musil's *The Confusions of Young Törless* are published by Penguin.

MICHAEL TANNER was educated in the RAF and at Cambridge University, where he was a Lecturer in Philosophy until 1997 and is a Fellow of Corpus Christi College. He is equally interested in philosophy, music and literature, his particular areas being Friedrich Nietzsche and Richard Wagner. He has written for many journals, contributed 'The Total Work of Art' to *The Wagner Companion*, and is the author of *Nietzsche* (1995) and *Wagner* (1996).

FRIEDRICH NIETZSCHE

THE BIRTH OF TRAGEDY

OUT OF THE SPIRIT OF MUSIC

TRANSLATED BY
Shaun Whiteside

EDITED BY
Michael Tanner

PENGUIN BOOKS

PENGUIN BOOKS

Published by the Penguin Group
Penguin Books Ltd, 80 Strand, London WC2R 0RL, England
Penguin Putnam Inc., 375 Hudson Street, New York, New York 10014, USA
Penguin Books Australia Ltd, 250 Camberwell Road, Camberwell, Victoria 3124, Australia
Penguin Books Canada Ltd, 10 Alcorn Avenue, Toronto, Ontario, Canada M4V 3B2
Penguin Books India (P) Ltd, 11 Community Centre, Panchsheel Park, New Delhi – 110 017, India
Penguin Books (NZ) Ltd, Cnr Rosedale and Airborne Roads, Albany, Auckland, New Zealand
Penguin Books (South Africa) (Pty) Ltd, 24 Sturdee Avenue, Rosebank 2196, South Africa

Penguin Books Ltd, Registered Offices: 80 Strand, London WC2R 0RL, England

www.penguin.com

This edition first published 1993

12

Typeset by Datix International Limited, Bungay, Suffolk
Set in 10/12 pt Monophoto Garamond
Printed in England by Clays Ltd, St Ives plc

CONTENTS

INTRODUCTION

I

The Birth of Tragedy (henceforth *BT*) was Friedrich Nietzsche's first book. The first edition, published on 2 January 1872, had as its full title *The Birth of Tragedy out of the Spirit of Music*, as did the second, very slightly revised edition of 1874. When he reissued it in 1886, Nietzsche renamed it *The Birth of Tragedy. Or: Greekhood and Pessimism. New Edition with an Attempt at a Self-Criticism*. The impact of its first publication was very considerable, though not, for the most part, in the way that Nietzsche could have hoped. Certainly its dedicatee, Richard Wagner, was thrilled by it, and wrote to Nietzsche: 'I have never read anything more beautiful than your book!', and Wagner's wife Cosima followed up with: 'You have summoned spirits in this book which I believed were only forthcoming at the behest of our Master.' Those reactions, and similar ones from Nietzsche's Wagnerian friends, were not surprising, in the light of the contents, especially of the later stretches of the work. But academic opinion was outraged, as was only to be expected, though it seems that Nietzsche had not anticipated it. An old enemy from his schooldays, Ulrich von Wilamowitz-Moellendorf, fired an initial salvo in May with the title *Philology of the Future! A Reply to Friedrich Nietzsche's Birth of Tragedy*, a piece of abusive academic polemic remarkable even by the standards that prevail in the world of scholarship. Nietzsche didn't reply himself, but his close friend Erwin Rohde weighed in with a rejoinder in the form of an open letter to Wagner, called *Afterphilologie!*, a difficult word to translate: it means, roughly, 'Pseudo-Philology', but *After* is also the German for 'arse', and there is a long tradition, not perhaps altogether unexpectedly stemming from Luther, of using the word in both senses simultaneously. Wagner, too, joined in the fight; and Wilamowitz continued the undignified squabble. Like all such battles, the outcome was indecisive, except that there was no doubt that Nietzsche had done himself a great deal of harm in professional circles, at the same time as he had decisively launched himself on the cultural scene.

As we shall see, when he came to write his 'Attempt at a Self-Criticism' in 1886, Nietzsche was far harsher on the book than any of his academic critics had been, their grounds for disapproval being only one element in the many-pronged critique he directs against the work. So what we now have is a bewildering whole, if we see it as that: the main body of the book is angrily denounced in the 'Attempt', at the same time as he tries to perform a rescue operation, claiming that in certain respects 'this impossible book' contains insights which he muddied by introducing jarring and incongruous elements, but which show that in certain crucial respects he was already on the main path of his life's work. It is, of course, a familiar tactic with authors looking with mixed feelings on their earliest productions, but in this case, more than usually, it presents questions about the nature of self-interpretation and development. What I shall do, in the first place, is to concentrate on the first edition, since that presents quite enough problems in itself, and then go on to deal with aspects of the 'Attempt' which are genuinely enlightening about what Nietzsche originally said, as opposed to what he later wished that he had said.

2

What kind of book is *BT*? That turns out to be so hard to answer that some commentators on it have concluded that it is *sui generis*, never a helpful category to invoke, since it provides one with no criteria for judging it by. The shortest answer is that, for all its brevity, it is a work which is attempting to do many things more or less simultaneously. The opening of the book proper is 'We shall have gained much for the science of aesthetics . . .', suggesting that what we are going to be offered, in line with the title, is a treatise on art, specifically on Greek tragedy. On the other hand, in the 'Preface to Richard Wagner', he refers to 'the seriously German problem that we are dealing with, a vortex and turning-point at the very centre of German hopes', and also to his conviction that 'art is the highest task and the truly metaphysical activity of this life'. So it would seem, and what follows bears this out, that Nietzsche has three major concerns (at least) going in tandem: a political-cultural one, a claim to be worked out about the nature of metaphysics, and a consideration of a specific phenomenon in the history of art. These were always to be central issues in his work, but what marks off *BT* as sharply different from (almost) everything that he wrote afterwards is its initially conventional mode of presentation, that of the academic essay. He had no notions at this stage of writing a disruptive work from within the establishment – as so often in his dealings with his contemporaries, he showed himself to be strikingly naïve about what the impact of his work would be. As a remarkably young professor of classical philology at a venerable university, he produced a work which met none of its criteria of respectability. Later on, he wrote work after work in which, now a freelance and in every way an outsider, he hoped to shake the world, and not only the world of learning, to its foundations, and no one took any notice. He soon came to characterize himself as 'untimely', but it took the shock of the reception of *BT* for the realization to strike him that in producing it he had been violently idiosyncratic.

The forces which were operating on him when he wrote the book were powerful and various enough for it to be a foregone conclusion that the result would be a weird hybrid. Like most people with a set of very strong passions, and a powerful urge to communicate them, he was convinced that they were intimately connected, that they proceeded from a central core of concern which the writing of a book would locate for his readers, and also for himself. Or still more strongly: he couldn't bear to think that he was in a serious way divided in his deepest self, whence these passions arose and which they also served to define. All his books, as he later came to insist, were reflections of his personal history – but then so are everyone's, he claimed: it was just that he was perspicacious and honest enough to realize a truth which almost all scholars, and especially philosophers, officially engaged in the disinterested pursuit of universal truths, insisted on denying. But when he wrote *BT* he was still a paid-up member of the club, so he presents his interests and views as ones which should be shared and accepted by his whole culture.

The three crucial elements in Nietzsche's intellectual make-up at the period when he was writing *BT* are very clearly apparent in the work itself. His training as a classical scholar engendered a profound love of Greek literature, equally of Homer and of the great tragedians of the fifth century BC, as well as a lifelong fascination with the philosophers, especially the pre-Socratics. But in 1865, when he was just twenty-one, he encountered Schopenhauer's philosophy for the first time, and the impact on him was intense, if not deep. He rapidly developed into a disciple, and since Schopenhauer's pessimistic world-view claimed validity independently of time or place, it was necessary to understand the Greeks in his terms. Four years previously he had got to know Wagner's *Tristan und Isolde*, after a fashion, in its piano reduction, and as an ambitious but untalented composer he fell utterly under its spell, and remained so for the rest of his life, as everything he wrote, from *BT* to *Ecce Homo*, his autobiography written in 1888 on the verge of madness, testifies.

These three enthusiasms were all at their peak when he wrote *BT*. What served to weld them together and to convince him that they were not only mutually illuminating but all parts of a unified, or at any rate unifiable, view of things was his friendship with Richard Wagner and Cosima. He was introduced to Wagner in November 1868 at the house of Hermann Brockhaus, Wagner's brother-in-law, in Leipzig. Wagner took to him immediately, and invited him to stay with him and Cosima, then still his mistress, in Tribschen, the house they were renting by Lake Lucerne. Nietzsche was dazzled by Wagner's charm, lack of condescension, humour and intimate knowledge of Schopenhauer's work. And Wagner was impressed by him, as a brilliant young classicist and someone who seemed to know some of his own music dramas well. From 1869, when Nietzsche took up his post at Basle, until 1872, when the Wagners moved to Bayreuth, Nietzsche visited Tribschen twenty-three times, sometimes for several days. And he was even honoured to be present for the first performance of the *Siegfried Idyll* on Christmas morning, 1870. At the end of his sane life, in 1888, he wrote in *Ecce Homo*: 'I offer all my other human relationships cheap; but at no price would I relinquish from my life the Tribschen days, those days of mutual confidences, of cheerfulness, of sublime incidents – of *profound* moments . . . I do not know what others may have experienced with Wagner: over *our* sky no cloud ever passed.' What he felt he had found in Wagner – and what he later vehemently denied was there to be found – was a reincarnation of the genius of Greek tragedy, combined with a deeply felt comprehension of Schopenhauer. However strong, independently of Wagner, Nietzsche's interest in Greek tragedy, its rise and decline, may have been, it was impossible for a person of his cast of mind to see the matter as one for purely historical investigation. It follows that the whole idea of the book must always have been permeated by Wagnerian influences, even if he wrote earlier versions of it – as he did – in which Wagner is not directly involved.

This, too, is a matter of more than scholarly concern. This highly peculiar book is thought by some to be a fascinating, original study which becomes polluted by Nietzsche's fanatical zeal for the Wagnerian cause from §16 to the end. A distinguished previous translator, Walter Kaufmann, has a note at the end of §15: 'The book might well end at this point – as the original did . . . The discussion of the birth and death of tragedy is finished in the main, and the following celebration of the rebirth of tragedy weakens the book and was shortly regretted by Nietzsche himself.' That is written from the standpoint of someone who not only had no interest in Wagner, the man or his work, but who wished that Nietzsche never had had either. Of course speculation as to the course of Nietzsche's thought if he had never been a Wagnerian is fruitless, but given that his primary concern was always with culture, its possibilities and catastrophes, it is not conceivable that he should have failed to be preoccupied with Wagner, even if he had never been a friend and intimate of his. He could not, under any circumstances, have remained an academic, given his temperament. At least as much as Marx, he was concerned to change the world, and held unswervingly the view that the health of a culture was to be estimated in terms of the art it produced. So an encounter of some kind between him and the most spectacular artistic presence of the nineteenth century was inevitable. It remains a matter for wonder that the kind and degree of intercourse between them should have been so intense.

That is not to deny that Wagner, always in need of propagandists, and especially once he had embarked on the Bayreuth project, must have been keen to see himself occupying a key position in *BT*, though in the long run it can have done little good to his cause. His admirers hardly needed Nietzsche's rhapsodies to enhance their devotion, while his detractors have always been inclined to take Kaufmann's line. Though it is true that the last third of *BT* is somewhat different in manner from the previous two-thirds, it doesn't strike a forced note, as the later *Untimely Meditation*, 'Richard Wagner in Bayreuth', written when Nietzsche was already having grave doubts about the whole subject, certainly does. But the shift in tone is inevitable: having given his account of the rise and fall of Greek tragedy, and the underlying reasons for it, he now has to explain to his audience how the rebirth is at hand, against all the odds. So the enterprise does become extended, and it is clear that Nietzsche is at something of a loss as to how to proceed. That is indicated by the enormous quotation from Schopenhauer, which has the effect, almost, of Nietzsche's reading aloud from *The World as Will and Representation* while he thinks of what to say next. The fact is that it must have become apparent to him at this point that his enthusiasms didn't fit together as comfortably as he had up to this stage been assuming, so he had to indulge in a mixture of analysis and rhetoric to create an impression of unity. The unity of intent on his part was there all along. But what he felt as a single complex of forces turned out to be recalcitrant to a discursive account. Hence, perhaps, the passage in the 'Attempt at a Self-Criticism', §3, which runs:

> What found expression here, in any case . . . was a *strange* voice, the disciple of a still 'unknown god', disguised beneath the scholar's hood, beneath the heaviness and dialectical joylessness of the German, even

beneath the bad manners of the Wagnerian; here was a spirit with strange, as yet nameless needs, a memory bursting with questions, experiences, mysteries, to which the name of Dionysus was appended as yet another question mark. This was the voice – they said suspiciously – of something like a mystical and almost maenadic soul, stammering laboriously and at random in a foreign tongue, almost unsure whether it wished to communicate or conceal. It should have been *singing*, this 'new soul', not speaking!

3

Nietzsche came to recognize, in other words, that the organization of *BT* was not what one would expect from a contribution to 'the science of aesthetics', but rather the expression of a set of intense reactions to art and the world, and really to the world seen as art. For what he congratulates himself for in the 'Attempt' is the formula which appears twice, slightly differently, in the body of the text: 'Only as an aesthetic phenomenon is existence and the world justified.' He has been criticized for introducing that formula without leading up to it in a logically impeccable way, but the point is that the whole work is suffused by that idea; that is its vision, and it wouldn't matter where it occurred, since it underpins everything that he has to say. It can be seen, in the first place and most lucidly, as an attack on the dominant account of tragedy which is the inheritance of Aristotle. In that tradition, tragedy improves us, both by giving us food for thought about such matters as hubris, and also, and most famously, by purging us of pity and terror, or through them. The world is interpreted in moral categories, and we see what to avoid and what to embrace. It is consonant with this view that Aristotle should have seen Euripides as 'the most tragic of the poets', and Aeschylus as the least, with Sophocles occupying a middle position. Nietzsche reverses the order: Aeschylus is the greatest, and Euripides is the agent of tragedy's 'suicide', to quote Nietzsche's lurid term. The lack, in *BT*, of almost any analysis of specific tragedies makes this assessment bewildering. Nietzsche seems to be standing so far back from the realities of Greek drama that it is only in the vaguest way that one can see why he should select as his hero someone whose sole surviving trilogy, the *Oresteia*, can hardly be regarded by us as a tragedy at all, ending, as it does, with the establishment of democracy in Athens, as a result of Apollo's casting vote in favour of Orestes. The elements that must have appealed to Nietzsche are, first, the fact that it *is* a trilogy, and Wagner was in the process of completing his own, influenced by the example of The Greeks – and also keener on Aeschylus than on the other two (The *Ring*, though in four parts, is called by Wagner 'a trilogy with a preliminary evening', since the first part, *Das Rheingold*, is primarily expository). Second, the chorus plays a much larger part in Aeschylus than in his successors. And third, and partly as a result of that fact, individual psychology is recessive in the *Oresteia*, 'myth' taking precedence.

It is in the contrast between 'myth' and 'psychology', though Nietzsche doesn't spell it out quite like that, that he sees the crucial difference between genuine tragedy and its counterfeit. He could never have granted the possibility of a tragic novel, for example. Myth re-enacts for us a story we all know, and in tragedy it does it in musical terms, though there is the problem, which Nietzsche later addresses, of what Greek music was like, since it is something of which we have little knowledge. But by affecting us at a level at which only music can, it enables us to come to an apprehension of the nature of what we are witnessing, which is, finally to introduce the most famous term of *BT*, Dionysiac. And once we begin to grasp the force of that term, and what it denotes, for Nietzsche, together with its complementary 'Apolline', we can begin to follow, if not to accept, his overall strategy, and see that he had ruthlessly to manipulate the material he was writing about in order to create his own meta-tragedy – a tragic story, but not a tragedy, since he hadn't sung it.

4

In crudest outline, and not following exactly the course of Nietzsche's wavery narrative: the Dionysiac and Apolline are in the first place forces, or categories in a metaphysical sense. In a way they are opposites, and Nietzsche, who was both attracted to dichotomies and intent on overcoming them (hence, perhaps, his claim in *Ecce Homo* that *BT* 'smells offensively Hegelian') does not regard them as mutually hostile, as many commentators think. They could not be, as soon as one sees what they actually come to. For the Dionysiac pertains to the nature of reality, while the Apolline is connected with modes of its appearance. Here Nietzsche is indulging in fully fledged metaphysics, derived, in some respects closely, from Schopenhauer. Like that arch-pessimist, he sees the essence of the world as consisting of a kind of metaphysical lava, composed of abstract willing, not that of any particular person, and not to any end; simply endless upheavals without goal or purpose. And like Schopenhauer, he sees the nature of willing as painful – here he relies on our ordinary concept, in which one wills something if one lacks it and wants it. But he has a still more flamboyant conception than Schopenhauer, since he talks of the primeval reality as a swirl of pain-cum-pleasure, though with pain always predominating.

If one protests that this hardly makes sense, that willing must belong to some agent, Nietzsche would agree; in dealing with reality we are forced to use our ordinary concepts in a monstrously extended way, since they are the only ones we have. So he means us to get a general idea of what he is talking about, but without pressing him for details, which he certainly doesn't provide. In this respect the metaphysics of *BT* are not in a notably worse position than those of many other metaphysicians, though instead of producing arguments for them, as say Plato or Spinoza had done, he is content merely to assert his view. Or that is how it strikes one at first. In fact the structure of *BT* in its metaphysical aspect resembles more what Kant had called a 'transcendental argument'. What Kant had meant by that confusing expression is something like this, in general terms: If something is the case, what else must be true to render that possible? In his great work *Critique of Pure Reason* Kant had proceeded largely by means of transcendental arguments to refute scepticism about the existence of a world in space and time, and of selves which experience it. In

BT the phenomenon that Nietzsche takes as needing explanation – an account of what makes it possible – is that of tragic pleasure. In other words, he is concerned with the question which has traditionally been posed as to why we enjoy portrayals of suffering on an enormous scale. Whereas the answer had been, since Aristotle, couched in psychological terms, Nietzsche finds them quite inadequate for the purpose. There is, he thinks (in *BT* and for a short time afterwards), something so striking about the difference between the pleasure we gain from the visual arts and epic poetry, on the one hand, and that which is vouchsafed us by music and tragic drama (which is properly speaking only that which is set to music) on the other, that we are forced to give an account of the fundamentally different drives which animate them. It is in this way that he comes to postulate the existence of the Apolline and the Dionysiac.

The pleasure of epic poetry or sculpture is to be accounted for by invoking our delight in appearances, especially if they partake of the lucidity of dreams. Everything in them has maximum individuality, the hardest edges. It is therefore illusory, since as Nietzsche has said, reality is one and indivisible. But during the pre-tragic age of the Greeks, when Homer told them the tales they needed to hear, they were consoled by being presented with a world which had separate heroes undergoing ordeals which were justified by the pleasure that the gods derived from watching them. Life may have felt tragic for men, but it was a divine comedy; and the grandeur of the Greek heroes is shown by their lack of resentment at being the entertainment of the gods. Fine as all that may have been, it was based on the postulation of a set of myths, in all senses of the word. What happened when epic was replaced by tragedy was that the principle of individuation (Schopenhauer's term, taken over for occasional use by Nietzsche) gave way to the chorus, apparent individuals submerging their identities in the mass. This is only possible under various unusual conditions – anyone used to academic surroundings will think immediately of rugger club dinners, an old Nazi will think nostalgically of torchlight processions in Nuremberg, and a member of a choral society of singing the finale of Beethoven's Ninth Symphony. These are all relevant to the state that Nietzsche describes, using the German *Rausch*, which roughly means intoxication. Clearly there are differences of quality to be noted among these conditions. But all of them are ways of putting us into closer contact with reality than we normally are – the superiority of some to others must be registered in terms of their effects. And it is in the experience of tragedy, as felt on both sides of the footlights (though it is desirable to dispense with those) that we gain the finest insight into the nature of the real. We learn the 'wisdom of Silenus', that 'The best of all things is something entirely outside your grasp: not to be born, not to *be*, to be *nothing*. But the second-best thing for you – is to die soon.' Or do we?

At this point it seems as if Nietzsche is espousing a pessimism as bleak as, if not identical with, Schopenhauer's. But he points out that, even when apprised of this dire wisdom, the Greeks, far from wanting to die, embraced life even more enthusiastically than before. How did they manage such a feat, and why, in any case, is it to be counted as a feat, as opposed to the absurdity of continuing with an existence which one knows can only be painful? The answer comes, as we have already seen, in two stages. First, the Greeks of Homer's time lived in order to entertain the gods: 'The same impulse that calls [Apolline] art into existence, the complement and apotheosis of existence, also created the Olympian world with which the Hellenic "will" held up a transfiguring mirror to itself.' Because the gods enjoy the spectacle of men suffering so much, noble men are eager to oblige: 'We might now reverse Silenus' wisdom to say of [the heroic Greeks]: "the worst thing of all for them would be to die soon, the second worst to die at all."' And Nietzsche immediately goes on to cite Achilles' lament over the brevity of existence.

It is a breathtaking move on Nietzsche's part to argue in this way; and whatever our objections to it may be, it makes clear that there is no question of Nietzsche's being opposed to Apollo. Such magnificent appearances, however much they may be illusory, justify themselves by their radiance. 'But how rarely is the naïve, that complete immersion in the beauty of illusion, achieved! How inexpressibly sublime, for that reason, is *Homer*, who, as an individual, is related to that Apolline folk culture as the individual dream artist is related to the dream faculties of the people and of nature in general,' Nietzsche continues. In the repeated stress on dreams and dream-states he is indicating that, for all its glory, this state must be impermanent. But while he concedes this, he reverses, explicitly, the usual order of preference between waking life and dreaming. 'The more aware I become of those omnipotent art impulses in nature, and find in them an ardent longing for illusion, and for redemption by illusion, the more I feel compelled to make the metaphysical assumption that the truly existent, the primal Oneness, eternally suffering and contradictory, also needs the delightful vision, the pleasurable illusion for its constant redemption.'

The Apolline in art, then, is the equivalent of the illusoriness of our usual state. We live in a condition of illusion, so dreams are 'the *illusion of illusion*', and none the worse for it. But illusions are of their nature unstable, and a people as restless in their search for the truth as the Greeks were bound to find that they could not rest content with them. The wisdom of Silenus reasserted itself, and they needed some further state, more penetrating and more all-embracing. The development of tragedy, in which the chorus was pre-eminent, even at first the only element, brought home to them the nature of the 'primal Oneness', and led them thus to rejoice in the destruction of the individual in the whole. That is the second stage in their coming to terms with existence. The same myths are employed in tragedy as in epic, but the tonality of the experience is radically changed. To be a pessimist in the conventional sense is not only cowardly but futile: there is no escaping the eternal agonizing drama of existence, so one exults in it, by ceasing, if only temporarily, to be *one*. If one attempts, as all philosophers have, even Schopenhauer, to give a moral justification of existence, the failure of the attempt will be embarrassingly evident, and refuge will have to be taken in ever-wilder imaginings to redeem our sufferings, which are inevitable and incurable. The moralist's plans for improving the lot of mankind by remedial action are like pissing in the sea. If one were to contrive simultaneously to preach a morality and to look unflinchingly at what the world is actually like, despair would be the only outcome. At the end of §7 Nietzsche puts the position in a nutshell:

> Understanding kills action, action depends on a veil of illusion – this is what Hamlet teaches us, not the stock interpretation of Hamlet as a John-a-dreams who, from too much reflection, from an excess of possibilities, so to speak, fails to act. Not reflection, not that! – True understanding, insight into the terrible truth, outweighs every motive for action, for Hamlet and Dionysiac man alike. No solace will be of any use from now on, longing passes over the world towards death, beyond the gods themselves; existence, radiantly reflected in the gods or in an immortal 'Beyond', is denied. Aware of truth from a single glimpse of it, all man can now see is the horror and absurdity of existence; now he understands the symbolism of Ophelia's fate, now he understands the wisdom of Silenus, the god of the woods: it repels him.
>
> Here, in this supreme menace to the will, there approaches a redeeming, healing enchantress – art. She alone can turn these thoughts of repulsion at the horror and absurdity of existence into ideas compatible with life: these are the *sublime* – the taming of horror through art; and *comedy* – the artistic release from the repellence of the absurd. The satyr chorus of the dithyramb is the salvation of Greek art; the frenzies described above were exhausted in the middle world of these Dionysiac elements.

The understanding that Hamlet possesses (though he can't be, in Nietzsche's terms, a character in a tragedy, since the eponymous drama has no music) is knowledge of the unalterable nature of things, and therefore to be dignified as 'wisdom', and opposed to mere 'knowledge'. In German the two terms are *Weisheit* and *Wissenschaft*. Tragedy is thus, for Nietzsche, a cognitive affair, though it moves us more than anything else does. We are transported by it to a state of wisdom, but it is presented to us in such a way that we react quite differently from Hamlet. He, so we might conclude, is confronted with the unappetizing Dionysiac truth neat, and so is bound to be destroyed. We encounter the Dionysiac truth in music, above all in the music of tragedy, in a way that makes it not only tolerable but irresistible. That is due to elaborate arrangements between the Dionysiac and the Apolline, which Nietzsche spells out at various places in *BT*, above all when he is considering Wagner later on. He does not achieve clarity, even complex clarity, on the subject, but it seems to me that the general idea is not too hard to grasp, whatever the inconsistencies and turgidities of its presentation. All art comes to us in some form or other, just as all experience is categorized ready for our consumption. That may mean that we never, so long as we survive our confrontations with truth, come into direct contact with it. Dionysus, as Nietzsche puts it in §21, speaks with the voice of Apollo, and finally Apollo speaks with the voice of Dionysus. In the end the deities, if we wish to see them as that, are collaborative when we achieve the full tragic experience. But Apollo is only present to the extent that he has to be. Tragedy, at its highest, is almost unendurable.

5

So strong men are needed not only to provide, but also to enjoy tragedy. The period during which they were able to turned out to be lamentably brief, though Nietzsche seems to think that that was due to misfortune rather than any historical necessity. What happened was that the third of the three Greek tragedians killed it by the production of works in which, though few have realized it, knowledge (*Wissenschaft*) was preferred to wisdom (*Weisheit*). This is signalized in Euripides' plays (for he is the villain) by the comparative insignificance of the chorus, and the multiplication of individual characters who think that they can resolve their conflicts by argument, or as Nietzsche puts it, dialectic. As soon as one puts one's faith in reason and reasoning, as opposed to intuition mediated through music, one has forfeited the possibility of genuine knowledge, which must always be tragic. Euripides was spurred on to this catastrophic achievement by the example, and perhaps the precept, of Socrates. And for many readers the climax of *BT* comes in §§11–15 of the book, where Nietzsche produces his account of how Socratism, a recurring phenomenon which has its purest expression in the figure after whom it is named, destroyed tragedy and set up the millennia-long belief in progress through reason, the monstrous equivalence of the true, the good and the beautiful, and the possibility of a total understanding and thus control of the world and of our own destinies. Historical accuracy, here even more than elsewhere in the book, may be at an ultimate discount. But the way in which Nietzsche presents his case is not only in itself beautiful and exciting, but certainly also convinces us of the existence of a type of outlook which is in the starkest contrast to that which Nietzsche calls Dionysiac.

For Nietzsche, every great positive manifestation of what is most valuable for human beings has a shady or at least inferior simulacrum. If the simulacrum is understood properly, it may be harmless or even indispensable. Thus in our ordinary waking state there is no doubt that reason and reasoning are valuable activities. But they pertain to the world of illusion, or appearance, and are powerless to instruct us as to the nature of the real. Aesthetic Socratism, Nietzsche's arch-foe at this first stage of his thinking, takes the opposite viewpoint; and the calamitous artistic result is that we have works in which we are fobbed off with pseudo-profundity, as can be seen from the inveterately optimistic attitude that they perpetrate.

> For who could fail to recognize the optimistic element in the dialectic, which rejoices at each conclusion and can breathe only in cool clarity and consciousness: that optimistic element which, once it had invaded tragedy, gradually overgrew its Dionysiac regions and forced it into self-destruction – its death-leap into bourgeois theatre. We need only consider the Socratic maxims: 'Virtue is knowledge, all sins arise from ignorance, the virtuous man is the happy man.' In these three basic optimistic formulae lies the death of tragedy. For now the virtuous hero must be dialectical, there must be a necessary, visible bond between virtue and knowledge, faith and morality; the transcendental justice of Aeschylus is reduced to the flat and impudent principle of 'poetic justice', with its usual *deus ex machina*.

It is a brilliant, and brilliantly presented case. And despite its wilfulness, in the presentation of a Socrates and Euripides whom in many respects we can hardly recognize, it strikes an echoing chord in anyone who is appalled by the superficiality of the routine moralistic claptrap about virtue, happiness and knowledge. But we must remember that it is all part of an argument which frequently gets submerged, but surfaces again and again, to the effect that if our tragic experiences – our experiences of tragic drama – are the most valuable we have, then the world must be constituted as Nietzsche claims. In the 'Attempt at a Self-Criticism' he stigmatizes the work as a piece of *Artisten-Metaphysik*, translated probably rightly, as 'artist's metaphysics'. That is, he admits that the book is 'romantic' in a sense that by the time he came to write the 'Attempt' he abhorred. To glorify art by seeing it as the way in which to discover truth struck him as perverse, and it may well be that it is. At the same time, it leads us to ponder on the nature of the relationship between our experience of suffering in life and in art in a uniquely intense way, so long as we are not so refrigerated by the book's hot flushes that we don't want anything to do with it. At every stage in his career Nietzsche was more concerned with what to do about the omnipresence of pain than about any other issue. As an extraordinarily sensitive person, and one who had little but suffering, both physical and psychological, visited on him throughout most of his adult life, he was naturally concerned that it should not dominate his thinking in a negative way. The lack of bitterness in his later writings, when he was in constant agony, is something to wonder at, whatever one thinks of their other aspects. But it almost seems as if life took the cruellest revenge on him for emphasizing, at the stage of his life when he wrote *BT*, and was personally happy and fulfilled, the amount of suffering that is always to be found in the world. For his descriptions of it in *BT* unquestionably possess a dimension of glamour which it is easy to find disgusting. They are notable for the armchair view he takes of the cosmic scene, as if what he is talking about is always something happening to someone else, almost always a mythical Greek hero. Yet by contemplating what they underwent he arrives at his formula that 'The world is only justified as an aesthetic phenomenon', with no implication that he is talking about anything less than everything.

The more he suffered himself, the more he became obsessed not with self-pity, of which he was conspicuously free, but with pity for others, obviously something to which he was forever in danger of submitting. His later works are silent, for most of the time, on how to cope with one's own pain, as if that were no problem, while they return time and again to the question of how to cope with the pain of others – pity for man is Zarathustra's last temptation, and we may take it that the near-identity of Zarathustra and Nietzsche is here at its most blatant.

6

But while everyone needs to cope with the issue of not being submerged in misery at the general state of the world, isn't it a monstrous solution to say that one mustn't try to alleviate it, but rather attempt to see it as beautiful? And, to repeat the point, isn't it something that would be said by a man who was relatively exempt from pain, and even primarily acquainted with it as he encountered it in works of art rather than in life? At this point Nietzsche does appear to be, for once, a child of his time, taking a Paterian view of things, or even the parodistic version of Pater to be found in W. H. Mallock's *The New Republic*, where the aesthete-figure says that the only thing requisite to complete the contemplation of Westminster Bridge at sunset is the sight of a poor unfortunate casting herself from the parapet into the Thames. It isn't even as if Nietzsche says, as he was soon to do, that some version of aestheticism is unavoidable if life is to be bearable; he talks of its being justified, and one might well ask: Who says that life is justified? Isn't such a claim a hangover from the view that it is morally justified, in supposing that it can be justified at all?

I don't know that a satisfying answer can be given to these questions, but it would be grievously unfair to Nietzsche to accuse him of simple callousness or even sadism. In the first place, his book was written to the greater glory of art, in particular tragedy, and the more he could pile on the agony of what art had to cope with, the more resplendent art became for succeeding in the task. And it isn't as if seeing the world as an aesthetic phenomenon is simply a matter of seeing it as one normally would and dubbing it 'art'. The suffering is transfigured by seeing it thus, though it might still be asked how much of a comfort that is to the sufferers. But that is a question that must be put to anyone who celebrates tragedy, and at least Nietzsche is not guilty of the humbug of talking about the affirmation of transcendent value resulting from the torments and deaths of individual characters. His whole account, it is difficult but essential always to remember, is predicated on a metaphysic which means that the categories we ordinarily apply to existence are illusory. Tragedy induces a state of intoxication in which we are not passive spectators of the 'witches' sabbath of existence', but participators, even if to some extent shielded ones, in the very mixture of ecstatic pain-cum-pleasure that, in its undifferentiated state, constitutes reality.

The shielding is done through the individuals who *are* destroyed by the immediacy of their contact with this ultimate truth of things. In a passage which reveals the centrality of the Wagnerian experience to Nietzsche's thinking on this whole subject, he asks whether one

> can imagine a man who could perceive the third act of *Tristan und Isolde*, unaided by word and image, simply as a tremendous symphonic movement, without expiring at the convulsive spreading of their souls' wings? How could such a man, having laid his ear against the heart of the universal will and felt the tumultuous lust for life as a thundering torrent or as a tiny, misty brook flowing into all the world's veins, fail to shatter into pieces all of a sudden? How can he bear, in the wretched bell-jar of human individuality, to hear the echo of innumerable cries of delight and woe from a 'wide space of the world's night' [a quotation from *Tristan*], without inexorably fleeing to his primal home amidst the piping of the pastoral metaphysical dance?

So we have the striking view that Tristan the character dies in Act Three of the drama because he has immediate awareness of the world's state, while he acts as a prism for us, through which the ecstatic pain is communicated. Or, to vary the image, Tristan dies that we may live. Tragic heroes are sacrificial victims, and we achieve 'redemption', a Wagnerian as well as Christian term that Nietzsche was soon to regret using, though he himself went on finding it handy, so long as nothing metaphysico-theological was intended by it.

It seems an extravagant claim, which would hardly survive

empirical testing. After all, orchestral rehearsals of *Tristan* without the tenor have occurred, and the auditors have survived to tell the tale. Furthermore, *Tristan* is, as everyone agrees, an extreme case, which admittedly does at the least make one feel very strange. What of all the purely instrumental music that we listen to without risking our lives, indeed with a sense of enhanced vitality? Yet Nietzsche does commit himself to the claim that almost all music, certainly all that is predominantly melodic and harmonic, is Dionysiac; only rhythmic music is Apolline. That too seems bizarre. In popular usage (derived from Nietzsche, but how debased?) a work such as Stravinsky's *Le Sacre du Printemps* would be much more likely to figure as Dionysiac than a late Brahms piano piece. The question does become acute of how far we can tolerate Nietzsche's seemingly wanton use of terms, and parade of almost lunatic exaggerations, in order to benefit from the spirit of what he has to say.

That question is to all intents what Nietzsche himself asks in the 'Attempt'. Indeed, it is the content of that remarkable piece of self-criticism which still manages to be covertly admiring to explore these very issues. How, Nietzsche is asking, can I possibly have committed myself to such a collection of shameful and embarrassing dogmas? He seems to be in that state of mind familiar to many teachers, who look at what they wrote a few years ago for their lecture course and are torn between wondering how anyone who wrote such nonsense can possibly ever have had a subsequent decent idea and pleasure that they have progressed so far that they can look back with wry amusement at their earlier efforts – those feelings, together with a slight sense that, for all the absurdity, they were getting at something which it is worth hanging on to, so long as they can shed the dross. Nietzsche rages at himself for having been the idolater of Schopenhauer and Wagner, with the implication that if one takes those two on board simultaneously what one is bound to end up doing is to multiply them by one another, the result being *BT*. There is a lot in that view. As soon as one spells out the fundamental ideas that are expressed in *BT*, the implausibility of many of them is manifest. Yet we find, as Nietzsche evidently did too, that it has a power which survives its poverty of argumentation, its clumsiness of formulation, and its refusal to countenance anything but extremes. It is no accident that it has maintained its status as one of the seminal books of the last century and a half. The very brutality of its simplifications has, no doubt unfairly, led to its fascinating people who are bored or bemused by more cautious works. For though it would be impossible, in the terms of the book itself, to call it Dionysiac, its momentum and general drift have a quality which brings it as close to that as a discursive work could come. Summary of it is defeating, not in the way that it is of Nietzsche's later works, which in a broad sense are aphoristic; whatever else, *BT* is not that. But it has a ferocity of conviction and exhilarating energy which put it in that small class of books in which the medium appears to dictate the message, or even to replace it. Few of its readers can give much in the way of an account of its detailed contents; few of them know, or care, about Wagner, or perhaps Greek tragedy. Nor are they in a position to assess the accuracy of the account of Socrates and his world-historical impact, as outlined in the book's centre. But its impact is none the less unforgettable for them, and to ask them how they have been affected by it is like asking how one has been affected by an overpowering piece of music. One can't say, or would be unwise to try. It is simply that one sees or feels things differently, at least for a time.

Does that mean that we shouldn't try to deal with its specific points, or assess its alleged insights? I don't think so, though there are three ways of approaching *BT* which strike me as attempting that in the wrong way. First, there are the commentators who work their way through it, pointing out where Nietzsche got it wrong, what can be salvaged and what has to be decisively jettisoned. That is to take *BT* seriously as history, and seems evidently foolish. Time and again Nietzsche stressed that when he referred to major figures he was using them as emblems for traits which he discerned in them, but which they did not necessarily have to anything like the extent, or in the pure form, which he attributed to them. While this sometimes is very misleading, as in the case of Euripides, what he goes on to say means that we can follow an argument about whatever subject Nietzsche is concerned with, using these proper names as no more than codes.

Second, there are those who approach *BT* with deconstructive techniques to hand, and therefore pay attention of such extreme thoroughness to the text that they are able to elicit many striking contradictions, revealing lacunae in argumentation, and so forth, which seem to them to show that, as usual, there is a layer, or series of layers, of meaning beneath or behind what Nietzsche wrote which demonstrate that the surface meaning is seriously misleading. While this procedure can, in some cases, yield valuable insights, I don't think that it does in this case. If Nietzsche had been attempting a rigorous analysis it would be a different matter. But it is so clear that *BT* is a work whose passion makes it slapdash that concentrating on its *ipsissima verba* seems merely a waste of effort. Various kinds of tact are needed in approaching texts, and the most basic kind is that which senses when a manifest content of a seemingly consistent nature is at odds with a latent content, which pokes through or fragments the pattern of perception that we are offered; and when, by contrast, the writing is the result of a state of excited and probably confused feeling and thought, where the most we can hope for is an account which preserves as much of the excitement as possible while admitting the confusion. In the very first sentence of the book, already quoted, Nietzsche writes of 'perceiving directly, and not only through logical reasoning, that art derives its continuous development from the duality of the *Apolline* and the *Dionysiac*'. This 'direct perception' amounts to Nietzsche's sense of the value of what he has seen, which is not a simple thing, but rather a rich mixture of his current enthusiasms. To examine in the minutest detail the language in which he struggles to articulate to himself what those amount to, involving, as it does for anyone engaged in such an enterprise, a great deal of pushing and pulling to get them into congruent shape, will only serve to evacuate the text of the kind of interest that it really holds, without replacing it with any other. I am not trying to excuse Nietzsche for writing slackly, only to point out that, since it is clear that the mode of presentation in *BT* is febrile and impressionistic, we had better accept it on those terms or leave it alone.

Third, we encounter the kind of commentary which is so intent on stressing the vertiginous complications of the work that it suggests that we ignore, so far as it is possible, the content and merely register the constant flux. On this view, it is virtually irrelevant to discuss what Nietzsche wrote, in the interests of the mode in which it is presented. I think that this is the least misleading way of mistreating *BT*, since the work is concerned to instil in us a sense of the primal chaotic oneness of being, and that is conveyed, up to a point, by abandoning ourselves to its vortex of confused intensities. But it can go too far. The contrasts which Nietzsche draws, even if they are not consistently held to, are still of enormous interest. No one who has not recently read *BT* is likely to be able to give an accurate account of it, since the confusions it contains are transmitted to its readers, and they then generate their own. So what one does is to remember some salient claims and concepts, but let the many specific twists of the argument retreat. In that respect, *BT* can stand for us as representative of many striking experiences, artistic, intellectual or other, that we have. This is treading on dangerous ground, since it looks as if it is permitting a degree of slackness which we wouldn't ordinarily tolerate. But then there is a great deal about *BT* which is only tolerable because of the exceptional quality of the central experience which those who fall in love with it treasure.

7

But once again, and for the last time, what is that experience – and to return to a question I asked early on, what are the terms in which *BT* is to be assessed? The best way to answer that question is to see it as a premonitory commentary on some famous lines of poetry that it surely inspired. They come at the beginning of Rilke's *Duino Elegies* (translation by Stephen Mitchell, slightly modified):

> For Beauty is nothing
> but the beginning of terror, which we are still just able to endure,

> and we are so awed by it because it serenely disdains
> to annihilate us.

The idea that beauty – one kind of beauty – should be so closely allied to terror is not new; or rather, the use of 'beauty' to cover what had traditionally been divided into the sublime and the beautiful *is* new, even while the terminology of Apollo and Dionysus might seem to be a loose fit for that distinction. But what makes the scheme of *BT* so endlessly fascinating and rewarding is the interactions between the two, whereas they had previously been treated as largely independent modes of experience. Beauty, in Nietzsche's early view, is both an intimation of the horror of life and a consolation for it. And it couldn't be the latter unless it was simultaneously the former. Art, at its greatest, tells the truth and makes it possible to bear it. Everything else in *BT* is subordinate to that idea, which is why it can survive so many criticisms, many of them of what appear to be central points. It is clear, for instance, that at the behest of a categorial scheme, Nietzsche badly overshot the mark in aligning the two artistic deities with forms of genres, in so absolute a way. He succumbed, in doing that, to his lifelong adoration of music. Because it was the art form that meant most to him – 'Without music, life would be a mistake,' he was to write in *Twilight of the Idols*, at the end of his career – he endowed it in general with the quality that he valued most in any art. No doubt his enthusiasm for Schopenhauer's aesthetics was also to blame: he got caught in a trap that Schopenhauer avoided only by dint of vagueness. If music is, by its very nature, the direct expression of the will, then it follows that it must unfailingly effect the transfiguration of the most intractable material. That is the core of *BT*'s 'artist's metaphysics'. We can resist it, and still find the claim that music, some music, perhaps Wagner's more than anyone else's, conveys experiences of elemental power and ecstasy. Whether that means that it has closer contact with reality is quite another matter, but it is natural to many of us, of whom Nietzsche is the exemplar, to think that it does. He spent the rest of his life wishing he hadn't been so extravagant, but, as often in metaphysics, without the extravagance we would almost certainly have been denied the insight.

As everyone agrees, during the nineteenth century the demands placed on art became progressively exorbitant. No one did more than Wagner to answer those demands, and no one did more than Nietzsche, for a brief period, to attempt to demonstrate how and why he had succeeded. Even so, the grandeur of each achievement is independent of the other, though if a person is immune to one it is unlikely that he will be enthralled by the other. But if one finds Wagner's intensities uncongenial, it is still possible to be stirred by the passionate metaphysics of Nietzsche's raw and brilliant first book.

Michael Tanner
Cambridge, September 1992

FURTHER READING

M. S. SILK and J. P. STERN: *Nietzsche on Tragedy*, Cambridge UP, 1981. This is a vast, compendious work on every aspect of *BT*, including the biographical background, its reception, both at the time and since, its relationship to earlier theories of tragedy, its 'plot', its account of ancient Greece, and its nature (including a critique). The book sustains its interest, while leaving one feeling that it has somehow omitted to deal with the central issues that *BT* raises.

WERNER J. DANNHAUSER: *Nietzsche's View of Socrates*, Cornell UP, 1974. Though it sounds as if it would only be dealing with one aspect of *BT*, if a central one, in fact the very long chapter on it covers many areas in sympathetic but critical depth and is extremely helpful.

PETER HELLER: *Dialectics and Nihilism*, University of Massachusetts Press, 1966. The forty pages Peter (not to be confused with Erich) Heller devotes to *BT* are a *tour de force* of brilliant exposition, in which the underlying hostility is cleverly disguised. Heller finds the drama of the book in its movement, not in what it actually says. It makes for an exciting read.

JULIAN YOUNG: *Nietzsche's Philosophy of Art*, Cambridge UP, 1992. This is an invigoratingly hostile account of Nietzsche in general and of *BT* in particular. Young lists his objections systematically, and defends them with an outraged sense of decency.

PAUL DE MAN: *Allegories of Reading*, Yale UP, 1979. The leading deconstructionist account of *BT*, which subjects it to an incredibly close reading, exposing to its author's satisfaction innumerable contradictions and 'aporias', i.e. points where insoluble problems are involuntarily produced. Dauntingly difficult reading.

HENRY STATEN: *Nietzsche's Voice*, Cornell UP, 1990. In the

Appendix to this extraordinarily brilliant book, Staten examines Paul de Man's critique of *BT* (see above) and subjects it, and another along similar lines by Philippe Lacoue-Labarthe, to a devastating deconstruction of his own, which leads, in a most satisfying way, to the reconstruction of *BT*. This is the *ne plus ultra* of usefully sophisticated reading.

THE BIRTH OF TRAGEDY

OUT OF THE SPIRIT OF MUSIC[1]

ATTEMPT AT A SELF-CRITICISM

I

Whatever it was that prompted this questionable book, it must have been a most important and attractive question, and a deeply personal one. This is borne out by the time in which – *in spite of* which – it was written, the exciting time of the Franco-Prussian War of 1870–71. While the thunders of the Battle of Wörth rolled away over Europe, the brooding lover of puzzles who was to be the father of this book sat in some corner of the Alps, brooding and puzzled – and hence both concerned and unconcerned – writing down his thoughts about the *Greeks* – the kernel of the strange and somewhat inaccessible book to which this belated preface (or postscript) will now be added. A few weeks later, and he himself was to be found beneath the walls of Metz, still struggling with the question mark that he had appended to the supposed 'cheerfulness' of the Greeks and Greek art; until at last, in a month of the most profound suspense, when peace was under debate in Versailles, he too made peace with himself and, slowly convalescing from an illness contracted in the field, gave definitive form to *The Birth of Tragedy out of the Spirit of Music*. Out of *music*? Music and tragedy? Greeks and the music of tragedy? Greeks and the pessimistic art form? The most accomplished, most beautiful, most universally envied race of mankind, those most capable of seducing us into life – they were the ones who *needed* tragedy? Or even more – art? What for? – Greek art? . . .

The reader might guess where the big question mark of the value of existence was raised. Is pessimism *inevitably* the sign of decline, decadence, waywardness, of wearied, enfeebled instincts? – As once it was with the Hindus, as it seems to be with us 'modern' Europeans? Is there a pessimism of *strength*? An intellectual predilection for what is hard, terrible, evil, problematic in existence, arising from well-being, overflowing health, the *abundance* of existence? Is it perhaps possible to suffer from overabundance? A tempting and challenging, sharp-eyed courage that *craves* the terrible as one craves the enemy, the worthy enemy, against whom it can test its strength? Wishing to learn from it the meaning of 'fear'?[2] What is the meaning, for those Greeks of the best, strongest, most courageous age, of the *tragic* myth? And of the tremendous phenomenon of the Dionysiac? And of the tragedy that was born from it? And on the other hand, that which brought about the death of tragedy: the Socratism of morality, the dialectics, modesty and cheerfulness of theoretical man – could not that very Socratism be a symptom of decline, fatigue, infection and the anarchical dissolution of the instincts? And might the 'Greek cheerfulness' of the later Greeks be nothing but the glow of sunset? The epicurean will *against* pessimism merely a precaution of the afflicted? And science itself,[3] our own science – what does all of science mean as a symptom of life? Might the scientific approach be nothing but fear, flight from pessimism? A subtle form of self-defence against – *the truth*? And, morally speaking, something like cowardice and falsehood? Amorally speaking, a piece of cunning? Oh Socrates, Socrates, was that, perhaps, *your* secret? Oh, secretive ironist, was that, perhaps, your – irony?

2

What I got hold of then, something terrible and dangerous, a problem with horns, not necessarily a bull exactly, but at any rate a *new* problem – today I should say that it was the *problem of science* itself – science seen for the first time as problematic and questionable. But the book in which my youthful courage and suspicion were then given vent – what an *impossible* book had to grow out of a task so unfavourable to youth! Constructed solely from precocious, excessively personal experiences, all close to the boundaries of communication, and presented within the context of *art* – given that the problem of science cannot be recognized within the context of science – a book, perhaps, for artists who also enjoy analytic and retrospective abilities (an exceptional kind of artist, then, who is not easy to find, but whom one has no great wish to find . . .), full of psychological innovations and artists' secrets, against the background of an artist's metaphysics; a youthful work full of youthful courage and youthful melancholy, independent, defiantly self-reliant even where it seems to yield to authority and respect of its own, in short, a 'first book', even in the worst senses of the term, racked with every youthful defect for all its old man's problems, terribly protracted and excitably portentous; on the other hand, given the success that it enjoyed (particularly with the great artist for whom it was intended as part of a dialogue, Richard Wagner), a *proven* book, by which I mean one that was good enough for 'the best minds of the day'. Accordingly it should be treated with a degree of discreet silence on my part. None the less, I should not like to suppress entirely how disagreeable it seems to me now, how strange it is to me sixteen years later – to an older eye, a hundred times more discriminating but no colder, no more alien to the task first tackled in this audacious book – *to see science under the lens of the artist, but art under the lens of life.*

3

To say it once again: today I find it an impossible book – badly written, clumsy and embarrassing, its images frenzied and confused, sentimental, in some places saccharine-sweet to the point of effeminacy, uneven in pace, lacking in any desire for logical purity, so sure of its convictions that it is above any need for proof, and even suspicious of the *propriety* of proof, a book for initiates, 'music' for those who have been baptized in the name of music and who are related from the first by their common and rare experiences of art, a shibboleth for first cousins *in artibus*[4] – an arrogant and fanatical book that wished from the start to exclude the *profanum vulgus*[5] of the 'educated' even more than the 'people'; but a book which, as its impact has shown and continues to show, has a strange knack of seeking out its fellow-revellers and enticing them on to new secret paths and dancing-places. What found expression here, in any case – and this was conceded with both curiosity and distaste – was a *strange* voice, the disciple of a still 'unknown god', disguised beneath the scholar's hood, beneath the heaviness and dialectical joylessness of the German, even beneath the bad manners of the Wagnerian; here was a spirit with strange, as yet nameless needs, a memory bursting with questions, experiences, mysteries, to which the name of Dionysus was appended as yet another question mark. This was the voice – they said suspiciously – of something like a mystical and almost maenadic soul, stammering laboriously and at random in a foreign tongue, almost unsure whether it wished to communicate or conceal. It should have been *singing*, this 'new soul', not speaking! What a shame that I dared not say what I had to say then as a poet: I might have been able to do it! Or at least as a philologist: – even today almost everything in this field still remains undiscovered and unexcavated by philologists! Especially the problem that there *is* a problem here – and that the Greeks, as long as we have no answer to the question 'what is Dionysiac?', will remain entirely unrecognized and unimaginable . . .[6]

4

So what is Dionysiac? This book contains an answer – 'one who knows' is speaking, the initiate and disciple of his god. Perhaps I would now be more discreet, less eloquent, in discussing such a difficult psychological question as the origin of tragedy among the Greeks. One fundamental question is the Greek relation to pain, their level of sensitivity – was that relation constant? Or did it radically change? – the question of whether their ever more intense *craving for beauty*, for festivals, entertainments, new cults, grew out of a lack, out of deprivation, melancholy, pain. If this is indeed so – and Pericles (or Thucydides) would lead us to believe as much in his great funeral oration – what would be the origin of the opposite craving that occurred earlier in time, the *craving for ugliness*; the good, rigid resolve of the older Greeks for pessimism, for the tragic myth, for the image of everything terrible, evil, cryptic, destructive and deadly underlying existence; what then would be the origin of tragedy? Perhaps *joy*, strength, overflowing health, excessive abundance? And what, then, would be the meaning, physiologically speaking, of that madness out of which both tragic and comic art arose, the Dionysiac madness? What? Is madness not necessarily, perhaps, the symptom of degeneracy, decline, of the final stage of a culture? Is there perhaps such a thing – a question for psychiatrists – as neuroses of *health*? Of the youth and youthfulness of a people? Where does that synthesis of god and goat, the satyr, point? What experience of himself, what impulse forced the Greek to imagine the Dionysiac reveller and primeval man as a satyr? And as regards the origin of the tragic chorus: in those centuries when the Greek body flourished, when the Greek soul overflowed with life, might paroxysms not have been endemic? Might visions and hallucinations not have been shared by whole communities, by whole cult gatherings? And what if the Greeks, precisely in the abundance of their youth, had the will *to* tragedy, if they were pessimists? If it was madness itself, to use a phrase of Plato's, that brought the *greatest* blessings upon Greece? And if, conversely, the Greeks, precisely at the point of their dissolution and weakness, became ever more optimistic, superficial, theatrical, more and more ardent for logic and a logical interpretation of the world, and thus both more 'cheerful' and more 'scientific'? What then? Might we not assume – in the face of all 'modern ideas' and prejudices of democratic taste – that the victory of *optimism*, the now predominant *reason*, practical and theoretical *utilitarianism*, like democracy itself, with which it is coeval, is a symptom of waning power, of approaching senescence, of physiological fatigue? And precisely *not* pessimism? Was Epicurus an optimist – precisely because he *suffered*? We can see what a heavy load of difficult questions this book has taken on – let us add its most difficult question! What, under the lens of *life*, is the meaning of morality? . . .

5

Already, in the preface to Richard Wagner, art – and *not* morality – is presented as the properly *metaphysical* activity of man; in the book itself, the suggestive principle is voiced a number of times, to the effect that the existence of the world is *justified* only as an aesthetic phenomenon. In fact, the entire book knows only one overt and implied artistic meaning behind all events – a 'god', if you will, but certainly only an entirely thoughtless and amoral artist-god, who in both creating and destroying, in doing both good and ill, wishes to experience that same joy and glory; who, creating worlds, rids himself of the *affliction* of abundance and *super-abundance*, of the *suffering* of his internal contradictions. The world: at every moment the *successful* redemption of God, the ever-changing, ever-new vision of the most afflicted, contrary, contradictory being, who can find redemption and deliverance only in *illusion*. We might deem the whole of this artist's metaphysic arbitrary, idle and fantastic – what is significant about it is that it already betrays a spirit which will defy all risks to oppose the *moral* interpretation and significance of existence. Here we see heralded, perhaps for the first time, a pessimism 'beyond good and evil', we see formulated that 'perversity of attitude' at which Schopenhauer never tired of hurling his most furious curses and thunderbolts – a philosophy that dares to demote morality and locate it in the phenomenal world, and not only among the 'phenomena' (in the technical sense of the term as used by the Idealists), but among the 'deceptions', as illusion, delusion, error, interpretation, artifice, art. Perhaps the profundity of this *counter-moral* tendency is best gauged by the discreet and hostile silence with which Christianity is treated[7] throughout the whole book – Christianity as the most extravagant elaboration of the moral theme that humanity has ever heard. Truly, nothing could be more opposed to the purely aesthetic interpretation and justification of the world as taught in this book than Christian doctrine, which is *only* moral, and seeks only to be moral, with its absolute standards: the truth of God, for example, which relegates art, *all* art, to the realm of *falsehood* – it denies, condemns and damns it. In this system of ideas and values, which must be hostile to art if it is to be in any way consistent with its principles, I had always sensed *hostility to life*, a furious, vindictive distaste for life itself: for all life is based on appearance, art, deception, point of view, the necessity of perspective and error. From the start Christianity was, essentially and fundamentally, the embodiment of disgust and antipathy for life, merely disguised, concealed, got up as the belief in an 'other' or a 'better' life. Hatred of the 'world', the condemnation of the emotions, the fear of beauty and sensuality, a transcendental world invented the better to slander this one, basically a yearning for non-existence, for repose until the 'sabbath of sabbaths' – all of this, along with Christianity's unconditional resolve to acknowledge *only* moral values, struck me as the most dangerous and sinister of all possible manifestations of a 'will to decline', at the very least a sign of the most profound affliction, fatigue, sullenness, exhaustion, impoverishment of life. For in the face of morality (particularly Christian, unconditional morality), life *must* constantly and inevitably be in the wrong, because life is something essentially amoral – in the end, crushed beneath the weight of contempt and eternal denial, life *must* be felt to be undesirable, valueless in itself. Morality itself – might morality not be a 'will to the denial of life', a secret instinct of annihilation, a principle of decay, trivialization, slander, the beginning of the end? And, hence, the danger to end all dangers? . . . So then, with this questionable book, my instinct, an affirmative instinct for life, turned *against* morality and invented a fundamentally opposite doctrine and valuation of life, purely artistic and *anti-Christian*. What should I call it? As a philologist and man of letters, I baptized it, not without a degree of licence – for who knows the true name of the Antichrist? – with the name of a Greek god: I called it the *Dionysiac*.

6

Is it clear what task I already dared to tackle with this book? . . . How I now regret that I did not then have the courage (or the immodesty?) to permit myself *a new language* as well, in all respects in keeping with such new ideas and risky innovations – that I toiled with Schopenhauerian and Kantian formulae to express strange and new valuations fundamentally opposed to the spirit and taste of Kant and Schopenhauer! What, after all, were Schopenhauer's ideas about tragedy? In the second part of his *World as Will and Representation*, he says: 'What gives everything tragic, whatever the form in which it appears, its characteristic tendency to the sublime, is the dawning of the knowledge that the world and life can give no true satisfaction, and are therefore not worth our attachment to them. It is in this that the tragic spirit consists; accordingly, it leads to resignation.' Ah, how differently Dionysus spoke to me! How far I was then from all that resignationism! – But the book contains something far worse, something that I now regret even more than having obscured and spoiled Dionysiac intimations with Schopenhauerian formulae: the fact that I *spoiled* the grandiose *Greek problem*, as I saw it, by adulterating it with the most modern ideas! That I introduced hopes where all was hopeless, where everything all too clearly indicated an ending! That I, on the basis of the most recent German music, began to fabulate about the 'German spirit', as if it were on the point of discovering, refinding itself – at a time when the German spirit, which not long before had had the will to conquer Europe, the strength to lead Europe, had, in its last will and testament, finally abdicated the task, under the pompous pretext of founding an empire, and was making the transition to mediocrity, democracy and 'modern ideas'! In the intervening period, in fact, I have learned to think hopelessly and mercilessly enough about that 'German spirit', and likewise about contemporary *German music*, which is romantic through and through, and the most un-Greek of all possible art forms; but also a narcotic of the worst kind, doubly dangerous to a people beloved of intoxication, which hails lack of clarity as a virtue, with its dual properties of being both an intoxicating and a befogging narcotic. – And yet – apart, of course, from all the impetuous hopes and applications to contemporary issues with which I spoiled my first book, the great Dionysiac question mark remains, also as regards music: how would a music be that was not romantic in origin, as German music is – but *Dionysiac*? . . .

7

But what, my good man, is romanticism if it is not *your* book? Can the profound hatred of 'the contemporary age', 'reality' and 'modern ideas' be taken further than it is in your artist's metaphysics – which would rather believe in Nothing, in the devil, than in 'the now'? Does a ground bass of anger and destructive rage not growl through all your contrapuntal, ear-seducing vocal art, a furious resolution against everything 'contemporary', a will that seems not too much removed from practical nihilism, and which seems to say: 'I would rather nothing were true than that *you* were right, that *your* truth should triumph!' Listen yourself, my dear pessimist, my dear idolater of art, with a more open ear, to a single passage taken from your book, that not uneloquent dragon-slaying passage which might sound insidiously pied-piperish to innocent young ears and hearts. Is that not the good old romantic credo of 1830, lurking behind the mask of the pessimism of 1850? And behind it, the introduction to the familiar romantic finale – break, breakdown, return and collapse before an old faith, before *the* old god . . . What? Is your pessimistic book not itself a piece of anti-Hellenism and romanticism; is it not itself something 'as intoxicating as it is befogging', a narcotic at any rate, even a piece of music, of *German* music? But listen:

Let us imagine a rising generation with such an undaunted gaze, with such a heroic proclivity for the tremendous. Let us imagine the bold stride of those dragon-slayers, the proud audacity with which they turn their backs on all the weaklings' doctrines that lie within that optimism, in order to 'live resolutely' in all that they do. *Must* the tragic man in that culture, trained through his self-education for seriousness and terror, not inevitably yearn for a new *art of metaphysical consolation*, tragedy, as his Helen, and to exclaim as Faust did:

> 'And should I not with utmost yearning seek
> To bring to life that creature most unique?'[8]

'Would it not be necessary?' No, thrice no! You young romantics: it would *not* be necessary! But it is very likely that it will *end up* like that, that *you* will end up like that, 'consoled', as it is written, for all your self-education in gravity and terror, 'metaphysically consoled'; in short, as romantics end up, *Christian* . . . No! You ought first to learn the art of *this-worldly* consolation – you should learn to *laugh*, my young friends, if you are determined to remain pessimists; perhaps as laughers you will consign all metaphysical consolations to the devil – and metaphysics in front of all the rest! Or, to say it in the language of the Dionysiac monster called *Zarathustra*:

Lift up your hearts, my brothers, high, higher! And don't forget your legs! Lift up your legs, too, good dancers, and even better: stand on your heads!

This laugher's crown, this rosary crown: but I myself put on this crown, I myself pronounced my laughter holy. I could find no one else today strong enough for that.

Zarathustra the dancer, Zarathustra the light one, who beckons with his wings, poised for flight, beckoning to all the birds, poised and ready, blissfully flighty.

Zarathustra the soothsayer, Zarathustra the soothlaugher, not impatient, not unconditional, who loves leaps and caprices; I crown myself with this crown!

This crown of the laugher, the rosary crown: to you, my brothers, I throw this crown! I pronounced laughter holy: you higher men, *learn* – to laugh!

(*Thus Spake Zarathustra*, Part IV, 'On the higher man')

Sils-Maria, Oberengadin
August 1886

PREFACE TO RICHARD WAGNER

In order to hold at bay all the possible scruples, agitations and misunderstandings that this book will create, given the singular character of our aesthetic public, and also in order to be able to write these introductory words with the same contemplative delight that marks every page, the concentration of good and elevating hours, I imagine the moment when you, my honoured friend, will receive this essay. How you, perhaps after an evening stroll in the winter snow, will consider the Prometheus Unbound on the title page, read my name, and be immediately convinced that, whatever this book may contain, the author has something serious and urgent to say, and also that he was communicating with you as the ideas came to him, as if you were a real presence, and was only able to write what was appropriate to your presence. You will recall that when your magnificent Beethoven *Festschrift* was published, amid the terrors and glories of the war that had just broken out, I was assembling my thoughts. But anyone who thought that this book reflected the contrast between patriotic excitement and aesthetic indulgence, between courageous seriousness and cheerful play, would be mistaken: were they really to read this essay, they would be astonished to discover the seriously German problem that we are dealing with, a vortex and a turning-point at the very centre of German hopes. But perhaps those same people will find it distasteful to see an aesthetic problem taken so seriously, if they can see art as nothing more than an entertaining irrelevance, an easily dispensable tinkle of bells next to the 'seriousness of life': as if no one was aware what this contrast with the 'seriousness of life' amounted to. Let these serious people know that I am convinced that art is the supreme task and the truly metaphysical activity of this life in the sense of that man, my noble champion on that path, to whom I dedicate this book.

Basle, end of 1871

THE BIRTH OF TRAGEDY

I

We shall have gained much for the science of aesthetics when we have succeeded in perceiving directly, and not only through logical reasoning, that art derives its continuous development from the duality of the *Apolline* and *Dionysiac*; just as the reproduction of species depends on the duality of the sexes, with its constant conflicts and only periodically intervening reconciliations. These terms are borrowed from the Greeks, who revealed the profound mysteries of their artistic doctrines to the discerning mind, not in concepts but in the vividly clear forms of their deities. To the two gods of art, Apollo and Dionysus, we owe our recognition that in the Greek world there is a tremendous opposition, as regards both origins and aims, between the Apolline art of the sculptor and the non-visual, Dionysiac art of music. These two very different tendencies walk side by side, usually in violent opposition to one another, inciting one another to ever more powerful births, perpetuating the struggle of the opposition only apparently bridged by the word 'art'; until, finally, by a metaphysical miracle of the Hellenic 'will', the two seem to be coupled, and in this coupling they seem at last to beget the work of art that is as Dionysiac as it is Apolline – Attic tragedy.

To reach a better understanding of these two tendencies, let us first conceive them as the separate art worlds of *dream* and *intoxication*, two physiological states which contrast similarly to the Apolline and the Dionysiac. It was in dreams, according to Lucretius, that the wondrous forms of the deities first appeared before the souls of men; in dreams that the great sculptor first saw the delightful bodies of superhuman beings; and the Hellenic poet, if questioned about the mysteries of poetic creation, would also have referred to dreams, and might have instructed his listeners much as Hans Sachs instructs us in *Die Meistersinger*:

It is the poet's task, my friend,
To note his dreams and comprehend.
Mankind's most true delusion seems
To be revealed to him in dreams:
All poesy and versification
Is merely dream interpretation.[9]

The beautiful illusion of the dream worlds, in the creation of which every man is a consummate artist, is the precondition of all visual art, and indeed, as we shall see, of an important amount of poetry. We take pleasure in the immediate apprehension of form, all shapes speak to us, and nothing is indifferent or unnecessary. But even when this dream reality is presented to us with the greatest intensity, we still have a glimmering awareness that it is an *illusion*. That is my experience, at least, and I could cite many proofs, including the statements of the poets, to vouch for its frequency, its normality. Men of philosophy even have a sense that beneath the reality in which we live there is hidden a second, quite different world, and that our own world is therefore an illusion; and Schopenhauer actually says that the gift of being able at times to see men and objects as mere phantoms or dream images is the mark of the philosophical capacity. Thus the man who is responsive to artistic stimuli reacts to the reality of dreams as does the philosopher to the reality of existence; he observes closely, and he enjoys his observation: for it is out of these images that he interprets life, out of these processes that he trains himself for life. It is not only pleasant and agreeable images that he experiences with such universal understanding: the serious, the gloomy, the sad and the profound, the sudden restraints, the mockeries of chance, fearful expectations, in short the whole 'divine comedy' of life, the Inferno included, passes before him, not only as a shadow-play – for he too lives and suffers through these scenes – and yet also not without that fleeting sense of illusion; and perhaps many, like myself, can remember calling out to themselves in encouragement, amid the perils and terrors of the dream, and with success: 'It is a dream! I want to dream on!' Just as I have often been told of people who have been able to continue one and the same dream over three and more successive nights: facts which clearly show that our innermost being, our common foundation, experiences dreams with profound pleasure and joyful necessity.

This same joyful necessity of dream experiences was also expressed by the Greeks in the figure of Apollo: Apollo, the deity of all plastic forces, is also the soothsaying god. Etymologically the 'shining one', the deity of light, he also holds sway over the beautiful illusion of the inner fantasy world. The higher truth, the perfection of these states in contrast to imperfectly comprehensible daily reality, the deep awareness of nature healing and helping in sleep and dreams, is at the same time the symbolic analogue of soothsaying powers and of art in general, through which life is made both possible and worth living. But our image of Apollo must incorporate the delicate line that the dream image may not overstep without becoming pathological, in which case illusion would deceive us as solid reality; it needs that restraining boundary, that freedom from wilder impulses, that sagacious calm of the sculptor god. His eye must be sunlike, as befits his origin; even should it rage and show displeasure, it still bears the solemnity of the beautiful illusion. And thus we might say of Apollo what Schopenhauer said of man caught up in the veil of Maya (*The World as Will and Representation* I [p. 352])[10]:

> Just as the boatman sits in his little boat, trusting to his fragile craft in a stormy sea which, boundless in every direction, rises and falls in howling, mountainous waves, so in the midst of a world full of suffering the individual man calmly sits, supported by and trusting the *principium individuationis.*[11]

Indeed, it might be said of Apollo that the unshaken faith in that *principium* and the peaceful stillness of the man caught up in it have found their most sublime expression in him, and we might even describe Apollo as the glorious divine image of the *principium individuationis*, from whose gestures and looks all the delight, wisdom and beauty of 'illusion' speak to us.

In the same passage Schopenhauer has described the tremendous *dread* that grips man when he suddenly loses his way amidst the cognitive forms of appearance, because the principle of sufficient reason, in one of its forms, seems suspended. If we add to this dread the blissful ecstasy which, prompted by the same fragmentation of the *principium individuationis*, rises up from man's innermost core, indeed from nature, we are vouchsafed a glimpse into the nature of the *Dionysiac*, most immediately understandable to us in the analogy of *intoxication*. Under the influence of the narcotic potion hymned by all primitive men and peoples, or in the powerful approach of spring, joyfully penetrating the whole of nature, those Dionysiac urges are awakened, and as they grow more intense, subjectivity becomes a complete forgetting of the self. In medieval Germany, too, the same Dionysiac power sent singing and dancing throngs, constantly increasing, wandering from place to place: in these dancers of Saint John and Saint Vitus we can recognize the Bacchic choruses of the Greeks, with their prehistory in Asia Minor, as far back as Babylon and the orgiastic Sacaea. Some people, either through a lack of experience or through obtuseness, turn away with pity or contempt from phenomena such as these as from 'folk diseases', bolstered by a sense of their own sanity; these poor creatures have no idea how blighted and ghostly this 'sanity' of theirs sounds when the glowing life of Dionysiac revellers thunders past them.

Not only is the bond between man and man sealed by the Dionysiac magic: alienated, hostile or subjugated nature, too, celebrates her reconciliation with her lost son, man. The earth gladly offers up her gifts, and the ferocious creatures of the cliffs and the desert peacefully draw near. The chariot of Dionysus is piled high with flowers and garlands; under its yoke stride tigers and panthers. If we were to turn Beethoven's 'Hymn of Joy'[12] into a painting, and not to restrain the imagination even as the multitudes bowed awestruck into the dust: this would bring us close to the Dionysiac. Now the slave is a free man, now all the rigid and hostile boundaries that distress, despotism or 'impudent fashion' have erected between man and man break down. Now, with the gospel of world harmony, each man feels himself not only united, reconciled, and at one with his neighbour, but *one* with him, as if the veil of Maya had been rent and now hung in rags before the mysterious primal Oneness.

Singing and dancing, man expresses himself as a member of a

higher community: he has forgotten how to walk and talk, and is about to fly dancing into the heavens. His gestures express enchantment. Just as the animals now speak, and the earth yields up milk and honey, he now gives voice to supernatural sounds: he feels like a god, he himself now walks about enraptured and elated as he saw the gods walk in dreams. Man is no longer an artist, he has become a work of art: the artistic power of the whole of nature reveals itself to the supreme gratification of the primal Oneness amidst the paroxysms of intoxication. The noblest clay, the most precious marble, man, is kneaded and hewn here, and to the chisel-blows of the Dionysiac world-artist there echoes the cry of the Eleusinian mysteries, 'Do you bow low, multitudes? Do you sense the Creator, world?'[13]

2

We have so far considered the Apolline, and its opposite, the Dionysiac, as artistic powers which spring from nature itself, *without the mediation of the human artist*, and in which nature's artistic urges are immediately and directly satisfied; on the one hand as the world of dream images, whose perfection is not at all dependent on the intellectual accomplishments or artistic culture of the individual; on the other as an ecstatic reality, which again pays no heed to the individual, but even seeks to destroy individuality and redeem it with a mystical sense of unity. Faced with these immediate artistic states in nature, every artist is an 'imitator' – either an Apolline dream artist or a Dionysiac ecstatic artist or else – as for example in Greek tragedy – a dream artist and an ecstatic artist at one and the same time. This is how we must imagine him as he sinks down, lonely and apart from the revelling choruses in Dionysiac drunkenness and mystical self-negation, as his own condition, his unity with the innermost core of the world is revealed to him *in a symbolic dream-image*.

Having established these general premises and oppositions, let us take a look at the *Greeks*, in order to assess to what degree and to what extent those *natural artistic impulses* were developed in them: this will lead us to a more profound understanding and appreciation of the Greek artist's relation to his archetypes; to quote Aristotle, 'the imitation of nature'. Despite all their dream literature and the many dream anecdotes, we can only surmise the nature of the *dreams* of the Greeks, but we can do so with a fair degree of assurance. Given the incredible accuracy of their eyes, with their brilliant and frank delight in colour, we can hardly refrain from assuming a logical causality of lines and contours, colours and groups that puts later generations to shame, a sequence of scenes like those in their best reliefs. Their perfection, if comparison is possible, would certainly justify us in describing the dreaming Greeks as Homers, and Homer as a dreaming Greek – in a more profound sense that than in which a modern man might compare himself in his dreaming with Shakespeare.

On the other hand, we do not need to rely on conjecture when we consider the massive chasm that separates the *Dionysiac Greeks* from the Dionysiac barbarians. From all corners of the ancient world – ignoring the modern world for the time being – from Rome to Babylon we can demonstrate the existence of Dionysiac festivals, which are at best related to the Greek festivals as the bearded satyr, deriving his name and attributes from the goat, is related to Dionysus himself. Almost universally, the centre of those festivals was an extravagant lack of sexual discipline, whose waves engulfed all the venerable rules of family life. The most savage beasts of nature were here unleashed, even that repellent mixture of lust and cruelty that I have always held to be a 'witch's brew'. It would seem that for some time, however, the Greeks were thoroughly secured and protected against the febrile excitements of these festivals, knowledge of which forced its way to the Greeks along every route of land and sea: the figure of Apollo rose up in all its pride and held out the Gorgon's head to the grotesque, barbaric Dionysiac, the most dangerous force it had to contend with. It was in Doric art that Apollo's majestically repudiating stance was immortalized.

This resistance became more questionable, even impossible,

when similar impulses emerged from the deepest roots of Greek culture. Now all the Delphic god could do was to disarm his powerful opponent of his destructive weapon by effecting a timely reconciliation – the most important moment in the history of Greek religion. Wherever we look we can observe the transformations wrought by this event. It was the reconciliation of two adversaries, clearly defining the boundaries that they were henceforward to respect, and periodically exchanging gifts of honour. Fundamentally the chasm had not been bridged. But if we consider how Dionysiac power revealed itself under the terms of that peace accord, and establish a comparison with the Babylonian Sacaea and its throwback of man to the condition of the tiger and the ape, we will be able to understand the meaning of those new festivals of world redemption and days of transfiguration. It was here that nature was first given its artistic celebration, here that the breakdown of the *principium individuationis* became an artistic phenomenon. That terrible 'witch's brew' of lust and cruelty had now lost its potency, and only the peculiar blend and duality of emotions amongst the Dionysiac revellers recalls it, as medicines recall deadly poisons – the phenomenon that pain is experienced as joy, that jubilation tears tormented cries from the breast. At the moment of supreme joy we hear the scream of horror or the yearning lamentation for something irrevocably lost. Those Greek festivals reveal a sentimental trait in nature, as though she were bemoaning her fragmentation into individuals. The chanting and gestures of these revellers, with their dual inspiration, was something new and unheard of in the Homeric and Greek world; and Dionysiac music in particular induced feelings of awe and terror. Music was apparently already known as an Apolline art, but only because of its rhythm, as regular as the sound of waves crashing against the shore, the creative power of which was developed for the representation of Apolline states. The music of Apollo was Doric architecture transmuted into sounds, but only into suggestive sounds such as those of the cithara. Care was taken to ensure that the one element held to be non-Apolline was excluded, the very element of which Dionysiac music consisted – the overwhelming power of sound, the unified flow of melody and the utterly incomparable world of harmony. In the Dionysiac dithyramb, man's symbolic faculties are roused to their supreme intensity: a feeling never before experienced is struggling for expression – the destruction of the veil of Maya, Oneness as the source of form, of nature itself. The essence of nature was now to find symbolic expression. A new world of symbols was required, the whole of the symbolism of the body, not only the symbolism of the mouth, the eye, the word, but the rhythmic motion of all the limbs of the body in the complete gesture of the dance. Then all the other symbolic forces, the forces of music – rhythm, dynamics and harmony – would suddenly find impetuous expression. In order to grasp this total liberation of all symbolic forces, man must already have reached that peak of self-negation that seeks symbolic expression in those powers: the dithyrambic votary of Dionysus is thus understood only by his fellows! With what astonishment the Apolline Greek must have looked upon him! And his astonishment would have been intensified by its combination with the terror, not in the end so strange to him, that his Apolline consciousness alone, like a veil, hid that Dionysiac world from his view.

3

In order to understand this we must level down, stone by stone, as it were, the elaborate construction of *Apolline culture* until we can see its underlying foundations. Only then will we be able to see the glorious *Olympian* figures of the gods standing on the gables of this structure, their actions, depicted in brilliant reliefs, ornamenting its friezes. If Apollo too stands among them, as one deity amongst others, without any claim to privileged status, we should not allow ourselves to be misled. The same impulse that is symbolized in Apollo gave birth to that entire Olympian world, and in this sense we may consider Apollo to be its father. What was the tremendous need that produced such a brilliant society of Olympian beings?

Anyone who approaches these Olympians with a different

religion in his heart, seeking elevated morals, even sanctity, ethereal spirituality, charity and mercy, will quickly be forced to turn his back upon them, discouraged and disappointed. Nothing here suggests asceticism, spirituality or duty – everything speaks of a rich and triumphant existence, in which everything is deified, whether it be good or evil. And thus the onlooker may be disquieted by this fantastic exuberance of life, wondering what magic potion these boisterous men must have drunk to enjoy life so much that, whichever way they look, Helen, 'floating in sweet sensuality', the ideal image of their own existence, smiles back at them. But we must call out to this onlooker, who has already turned his back: go not, but first hear what Greek folk wisdom says of this same life, spread out before you here with such inexplicable cheerfulness. According to the old story, King Midas had long hunted wise *Silenus*, Dionysus' companion, without catching him. When Silenus had finally fallen into his clutches, the king asked him what was the best and most desirable thing of all for mankind. The daemon stood silent, stiff and motionless, until at last, forced by the king, he gave a shrill laugh and spoke these words: 'Miserable, ephemeral race, children of hazard and hardship, why do you force me to say what it would be much more fruitful for you not to hear? The best of all things is something entirely outside your grasp: not to be born, not to *be*, to be *nothing*. But the second-best thing for you – is to die soon.'

How does this folk wisdom relate to the Olympian world of the gods? As does the ecstatic vision of the tortured martyr to his torments.

Now the Olympian magic mountain opens up before us, revealing all its roots. The Greeks knew and felt the fears and horrors of existence: in order to be able to live at all they had to interpose the radiant dream-birth of the Olympians between themselves and those horrors. The terrible mistrust of the Titanic forces of nature; the Moira mercilessly reigning over all man's knowledge; the vultures that tormented the great friend to man, Prometheus; the terrible destiny of wise Oedipus; the family curse of the Atreids, forcing Orestes to matricide – in short the entire philosophy of the god of the woods, along with its mythical examples, which brought about the downfall of the gloomy Etruscans – the Greeks repeatedly overcame all this, or at least veiled and concealed it, with the artistic *middle world* of the Olympians. In order to live, the Greeks were profoundly compelled to create those gods. We might imagine their origin as follows; the Apolline impulse to beauty led, in gradual stages, from the original Titanic order of the gods of fear to the Olympian order of the gods of joy, just as roses sprout on thorn-bushes. How else could life have been borne by a race so sensitive, so impetuous in its desires, so uniquely capable of *suffering*, if it had not been revealed to them, haloed in a higher glory, in their gods? The same impulse that calls art into existence, the complement and apotheosis of existence, also created the Olympian world with which the Hellenic 'will' held up a transfiguring mirror to itself. Thus the gods provide a justification for the life of man by living it themselves – the only satisfactory form of theodicy! Existence under the bright sunlight of gods such as these was felt to be the highest goal of mankind, and the true grief felt by Homeric man came from departure from it, especially when that departure was near. We might now reverse Silenus' wisdom to say of them: 'the worst thing of all for them would be to die soon, the second worst to die at all'. If this lament is voiced once, it is heard again . . . from short-lived Achilles, mourning the leaf-like change and transformation of the human race, the collapse of the heroic age. It is not unworthy of the greatest of all heroes to long for a continuation of life, even as a day labourer. The 'will', at the Apolline stage, longs so impetuously for life, and Homeric man feels so at one with it that even lamentation becomes his song of praise.

Here we must point out that the harmony that men of more recent times have so yearned for, indeed the unity of man with nature, to which Schiller applied the artistic word 'naïve',[14] is by no means such a simple, obvious, inevitable state that we would *necessarily* encounter it at the gateway to every culture, as a paradise of humanity. The only era that could hold such a view would be one that saw Rousseau's Émile as an artist, and deluded itself that in Homer it had found just such an artist-Émile, reared at nature's breast. Whenever we encounter the naïve in art, we should recognize that we are in the presence of the highest impact of Apolline culture, which must always overthrow a realm of Titans and slay monsters, and which must emerge triumphant over a terrible abyss in its contemplation of the world and its most intense capacity for suffering, by resorting to the most powerful and pleasurable illusions. But how rarely is the naïve, that complete immersion in the beauty of illusion, achieved! How inexpressibly sublime, for that reason, is *Homer*, who, as an individual, is related to that Apolline folk culture as the individual dream artist is related to the dream faculties of the people and of nature in general. Homeric *naïveté* can only be understood as the complete triumph of Apolline illusion: this is one of those illusions that nature so often uses in order to attain its goals. The true goal is veiled by a phantasm: we stretch our hands towards one thing, and nature deceives us to achieve the other. Amongst the Greeks the 'will' wished to contemplate itself, in the transfiguration of genius and the world of art; in order to glorify themselves, its creations had to feel worthy of glorification, they had to see themselves in a higher sphere, without this contemplation seeming either a command or a reproach. It was in this sphere of beauty that they saw reflections of themselves, the Olympians. With this reflection of beauty the Hellenic 'will' battled with the talent, correlative to the artistic talent, for suffering and the wisdom of suffering, and as a monument to its triumph stands Homer, the naïve artist.

4

The dream analogy may tell us something about this naïve artist. Let us recall the dreamer and the way, in the midst of the illusion of the dream world and without disturbing it, he calls out to himself: 'It is a dream! I want to dream on!' If we must conclude from this a deep inner delight in the contemplation of dreams, or if, on the other hand, before we can dream with that inner delight in contemplation we must first completely erase the day and its terrible intrusiveness, we may interpret all these phenomena more or less as follows, guided by Apollo, the interpreter of dreams.

Although of life's two halves – waking and sleeping – the former is held to be preferable, more important, more considerable and more worth living, indeed the only one that *is* lived, I should still, paradoxical as it may sound, like to maintain the opposite valuation of the dream in relation to the mysterious foundation of our being, whose phenomena we are. The more aware I become of those omnipotent art impulses in nature, and find in them an ardent longing for illusion and for redemption by illusion, the more I feel compelled to make the metaphysical assumption that the truly existent, the primal Oneness, eternally suffering and contradictory, also needs the delightful vision, the pleasurable illusion for its constant redemption: an illusion that we, utterly caught up in it and consisting of it – as a continuous becoming in time, space and causality, in other words – are required to see as empirical reality. If we look away from our own 'reality', then, for a moment, if we see our empirical existence, like that of the world in general, as an idea of the primal Oneness created in a moment, then we must see the dream as the *illusion of illusion*,[15] and hence as an even higher satisfaction of the original desire for illusion. It is for the same reason that the innermost core of nature takes such unutterable delight in the naïve artist and the naïve work of art, which is likewise only 'the illusion of illusion'. *Raphael*, himself one of those immortal naïves, in one of his allegorical paintings depicted that reduction of illusion to mere illusion, the original act of the naïve artist and also of Apolline culture. In his *Transfiguration*, the lower half of the painting, with the possessed boy, his despairing bearers, the dismayed and terrified disciples, reveals the reflection of eternal, primal suffering, the sole foundation of the world: 'illusion' here is the reflection of the eternal contradiction, of the father of all things. From this illusion there now arises, like an ambrosial vapour, a new and visionary world of illusion of which those caught up in the first illusion see nothing – a radiant floating in the purest bliss and painless contemplation beaming from wide-open eyes. Here, in the highest artistic symbolism, we behold that Apolline world of beauty and its substratum, the terrible wisdom of Silenus, and we intuitively understand their reciprocal necessity. Apollo, however, appears to us once again as the apotheosis of the *principium individuationis*. Only through him does the perpetually attained goal of primal Oneness, redemption through illusion, reach consummation. With sublime gestures he reveals to us how the whole world of torment is necessary so that the individual can create the redeeming vision, and then, immersed in contemplation of it, sit peacefully in his tossing boat amid the waves.

If it can be seen as at all imperative and prescriptive, this deification of individuation knows but a single law, the individual; that is, the maintenance of the boundaries of the individual, *moderation* in the Hellenic sense. Apollo, as an ethical deity, demands moderation from his followers and, in order to maintain it, self-knowledge. And thus the admonitions 'Know thyself' and 'Nothing to excess!' coexist with the aesthetic necessity of beauty, while hubris and excess are considered the truly hostile spirits of the non-Apolline realm, and hence qualities of the pre-Apolline age, the age of the Titans, and the world beyond the Apolline, the world of the barbarians. It was for his Titanic love of man that Prometheus had to be torn apart by vultures; for his excessive wisdom in solving the riddle of the Sphinx that Oedipus had to be cast into a bewildering vortex of crimes: thus did the Delphic god interpret the Greek past.

The Apolline Greeks also saw the effect of the *Dionysiac* as 'Titanic' and 'barbaric', unable to conceal from themselves the fact that they themselves were also inwardly akin to those fallen Titans and heroes. Indeed, they were forced to feel even more than that: their entire existence, with all its beauty and moderation, was based on a veiled substratum of suffering and knowledge, revealed to them once again by the Dionysiac. And behold! Apollo could not live without Dionysus! The 'Titanic' and the 'barbaric' were, in the end, just as necessary as the Apolline! And let us now imagine how the ecstatic sound of the Dionysiac revels echoed ever more enticingly around this world, built on illusion and *moderation*, and artificially restrained – how their clamour voiced all the *excess* of nature in delight, suffering and knowledge, and even in the most piercing cry: imagine what the psalmodizing Apolline artist, with his phantom harp-notes, could have meant compared to this daemonic folk song! The muses of the arts of 'illusion' blanched before an art that voiced the truth in its intoxication – the wisdom of Silenus cried 'Woe! Woe!' to the cheerful Olympians. The individual, with all his restraints and moderations, was submerged in the self-oblivion of the Dionysiac state and forgot the Apolline dictates. *Excess* was revealed as truth, contradiction; the bliss born of pain spoke from the heart of nature. And consequently, wherever the Dionysiac invasion was successful, the Apollonian was negated and destroyed. But just as certain is it that where the first onslaught was successfully withstood, the esteem and majesty of the Delphic god was expressed more rigidly and more threateningly than ever. In fact, I can explain the *Doric* state and Doric art only as a continued encampment of the Apolline; only unstinting resistance to the Titanic and barbaric essence of the Dionysiac could explain the long-term survival of such a scornfully remote art, so enclosed in bulwarks, such a warlike and severe training, such a cruel and ruthless state.

I have up until this point expanded on the observation I made at the beginning: how the Dionysiac and the Apolline, in a sequence of renewed births, mutually intensifying one another, dominated the nature of Greece: how the Homeric world developed out of the 'bronze age', with its Titanic battles and its stern popular philosophy, under the constraints of the Apolline impulse to beauty; how this naïve magnificence was engulfed once more by the encroaching Dionysiac flood, and how, in the face of this new power, the Apolline rose to the rigid majesty of Doric art and the Doric view of the world. If the older Greek history falls into four major artistic stages in the battle between these two hostile principles, we must inquire into the final goal of this process of development, lest we see the final period reached, the period of Doric art, as the summit and goal of those artistic impulses. And now we can see the sublime and esteemed work of art that is *Attic tragedy* and the dramatic dithyramb as the common goal of the two impulses, whose mysterious marriage, after a long period of early strife, was finally blessed with such a child, at once Antigone and Cassandra.

5

We are now approaching the true goal of our inquiry: that of understanding the Dionysiac-Apolline genius and its works of art, or at least gaining a sense of the mystery of that union. Now we shall first of all ask ourselves: where in the Hellenic world did that seed first appear which later grew into tragedy and the dramatic dithyramb? The ancient world itself gives us a pictorial answer, presenting the forefathers and torch-bearers of Greek poetry, *Homer* and *Archilochus*, side by side on sculptures, gemstones and so on, in the certain belief that these two alone were worthy of respect, both of them completely and equally original, from whom there issued a stream of fire that flowed over the whole of the later Greek world. Homer, the aged, self-absorbed dreamer, the prototype of the Apolline naïve artist, is now astonished to behold the passionate head of the warlike votary of the muses, driven wildly through life; and the new aesthetic has been able to contribute only the interpretation that here the 'objective' artist stood face to face with the first 'subjective' artist. This interpretation is of little use to us, because we know the subjective artist only as a bad artist, and throughout the whole of art we demand above all else the conquest of the subjective, release from the 'self', and the silencing of all individual will and craving; indeed we cannot imagine a truly artistic creation, however unimportant, without objectivity, without a pure and disinterested contemplation.[16] For this reason our aesthetic must first resolve the problem of how it is possible to consider the 'lyric poet' as an artist: he who, in the experience of all ages, always says 'I' and sings us through the full chromatic scale of his passions and desires. It is this Archilochus who frightens us, as he stands next to Homer, with the cry of his hate and scorn, the drunken outpourings of his desire; is he, the first artist to be termed 'subjective', not consequently the true non-artist? How, then, did he win the honour bestowed upon him by the Delphic oracle, the home of 'objective' art, in a number of highly remarkable sayings?

Schiller cast some light on the process of writing his poetry in a psychological observation that he himself found inexplicable but which did not give him pause. In the state prior to the act of writing, he does not claim to have had before or within him an ordered causality of ideas, but rather a *musical mood*. ('For me, feeling does not at first have a clearly defined object. This is only formed later on. A certain musical atmosphere of moods precedes it, and the poetic idea only comes afterwards.') If we add to that the most important phenomenon in the whole of ancient poetry, the unification, or indeed the identity – which they assumed to be quite natural – of the *lyric poet with the musician*, compared to which our more modern lyric poetry appears as the headless statue of a god, we can now use the artist's metaphysics described above to explain the lyric poet as follows. First of all, as a Dionysiac artist, he has been thoroughly united with the primal Oneness, its pain and contradiction, and produces the copy of that primal Oneness as music, if we can rightly call music a repetition and recast of the world; but now, under the Apolline dream influence, this music is revealed to him as an *allegorical dream-image*. That reflection of primal pain in music, free of images and concepts, redeemed by illusion, now creates a second mirror image as a single allegory or example. The artist has already abandoned his subjectivity in the Dionysiac process: the image that now reveals to him his unity with the heart of the world is a dream scene symbolizing the primal contradiction and primal suffering, as well as the primal delight in illusion. The 'I' of the lyric poet therefore sounds from the very depths of being: his 'subjectivity' in the sense used by modern aestheticians is a falsehood. When Archilochus, the first lyric poet among the Greeks, proclaims his raging love and at the same time his contempt for the daughters of Lycambes, it is not his passion that dances before us in orgiastic frenzy: we see Dionysus and the Maenads, we see the intoxicated reveller Archilochus sunk in sleep – as Euripides describes it in the *Bacchae*, asleep in a high mountain pasture in the midday sun – and now Apollo comes up to him and touches him with the laurel. The Dionysiac musical enchantment of the sleeping man now sends out sparks of images, lyric poems which, at the peak of their evolution, will bear the name of tragedies and dramatic dithyrambs.

The sculptor, like his close kin the epic poet, has lost himself in pure contemplation of images. Without a single image, the Dionysiac musician is himself nothing but primal suffering and its primal resonance. The lyric genius is aware of a world of images and symbols growing out of this mystical state of self-expression and unity, one that is utterly different in colouring, causality and tempo from the world of the sculptor and epic poet. While the latter lives with joyful ease within these images and only within them, and never tires of lovingly contemplating them down to the minutest detail; while he sees even the image of the raging Achilles as a mere illusion whose raging expression he enjoys with that dreaming delight in illusion, so that this mirror of illusion guards him against becoming as one and fusing with his figures; the lyric poet's images are nothing but the poet himself, and only different objectifications of himself, which is why, as the moving centre of that world, he is able to say 'I': this self is not that of the waking, empirically real man, however, but rather the sole, truly existing and eternal self that dwells at the basis of being, through whose depictions the lyric genius sees right through to the very basis of being. Let us now consider how, amongst these depictions, he also sees *himself* as a non-genius, as his 'subject', the whole horde of subjective passions and stirrings of the will directed at a particular object that seems real to him; if it now appears that the lyric genius and the non-genius connected to him are one, and that the former is using that little word 'I' to refer to himself, this illusion will no longer have the power of seducing us, as it has certainly seduced those who have described the lyric poet as the subjective poet. In fact Archilochus the man, consumed with passion, loving and hating, is only a vision of the genius who has already ceased to be Archilochus and instead becomes the world-genius, and who symbolically expresses his primal pain in that symbol of the man Archilochus: while that subjectively craving and desiring man Archilochus can never, ever be a poet. But it is not at all necessary for the lyric poet to see only the phenomenon of the man Archilochus before him as the reflection of eternal being; and tragedy proves how remote the visionary world of the lyric poet can be from that most immediate phenomenon.

Schopenhauer, who did not conceal from himself the difficulty presented by the lyric poet when it comes to the philosophical consideration of art, believes that he has found an escape route along which I cannot follow him. He alone, in his profound metaphysics of music, has been given the means to achieve a solution. I hope that I have here resolved those same difficulties according to his spirit and his honour. However, he described the singular essence of song as follows:

> It is the subject of the will, that is, his own willing, that fills the singer's consciousness, often as an unbound and satisfied willing (joy), but even more often as a hampered willing (sorrow), always as emotion, passion, an agitated state of mind. Beside this, however, and simultaneously with it, the singer, through the sight of surrounding nature, becomes aware of himself as the subject of pure, will-less knowing, whose unshakeable, blissful peace now appears in contrast to the pressure of willing, always restricted and needy. The feeling of this contrast, this alternate play, is really what is being expressed in the whole of the song, and what constitutes the lyrical state in general. In this state pure knowing comes to us, as it were, in order to deliver us from willing and its pressure. We follow, but only for a few moments; willing, desire, the recollection of our own personal aims, always tears us away again from peaceful contemplation; but again and again the next beautiful surroundings, in which pure, will-less knowledge presents itself to us, entice us away from willing. Therefore in the song and in the lyrical mood, willing (the personal interest of our aims) and pure perception of the surroundings that present themselves are wonderfully blended with each other. Relations between the two are sought and imagined; the subjective mood, the affection of the will, imparts its colour to the perceived environment, and the environment imparts its own to the mood. The genuine song is the copy or impression of the whole of this mingled and divided state of mind.
>
> (*The World as Will and Representation*, I [p. 250])

Who could fail to understand that in this description lyric poetry is being characterized as an incompletely achieved art that seldom reaches its goal, and then only by means of a leap – a half-art, whose *essence* lies in the miraculous fusing of willing and pure contemplation, the non-aesthetic and the aesthetic states? We insist, instead, that the opposition of the subjective and the objective, which Schopenhauer employs as a yardstick in his classification of the arts, has no place in aesthetics, since the subject, the individual who wills and furthers his own egoistic purposes, can be considered only the adversary and not the origin of art. But in so far as the subject is an artist, he is already liberated from his individual will and has become a medium through which the only truly existent subject celebrates his redemption through illusion. For this above all must be plain to us, to our humiliation *and* our enhancement, that the whole comedy of art is not at all performed for us, for our improvement or edification, any more than we are the actual creators of that art world: but we can indeed assume for our own part that we are images and artistic projections for the true creator of that world, and that our highest dignity lies in the meaning of works of art – for it is only as *an aesthetic phenomenon* that existence and the world are eternally *justified*[17] – while of course our awareness of our meaning differs hardly at all from the awareness that warriors painted on canvas have of the battle portrayed. Thus all of our knowledge of art is utterly illusory, because we, as knowing subjects, are not identical with that being which, as sole creator and spectator of that comedy of art, prepares an eternal enjoyment for itself. Only in so far as the genius is fused with the primal artist of the world in the act of artistic creation does he know anything of the eternal essence of art; for in that state he is wonderfully similar to the weird fairy-tale image of the creature than can turn its eyes around and look at itself; now he is at once subject and object, at once poet, actor and audience.

6

As regards Archilochus, learned research has revealed that he introduced the *folk song* into literature, and that for this deed he was accorded his unique place beside Homer in the universal estimation of the Greeks. But what is the folk song as distinct from the utterly Apolline epos? What is it but the *perpetuum vestigium* of a unification of the Apolline and the Dionysiac? Its tremendously wide dissemination amongst all peoples, intensified in constantly new manifestations, tells us of the strength of nature's dual artistic impulse, which leaves its trace in the folk song just as the orgiastic movements of a people are immortalized in its music. Indeed, it must also be historically demonstrable that any period richly productive of folk songs has also been most intensely stimulated by Dionysiac currents, which we must always see as the substratum and precondition for the folk song.

But first of all we must see the folk song as a musical mirror to the world, the original melody, which now seeks a parallel manifestation in dream and expresses it in poetry. *Melody, then, is both primary and universal*, which is why it can therefore bear various objectifications in various texts. It is also more important and necessary by far in the naïve estimation of the people. Melody gives birth to poetry, over and over again; this is precisely what *the strophic form of the folk song* tells us: a phenomenon that always astonished me, until I finally hit upon this explanation. If we consider a collection of folk songs such as *Des Knaben Wunderhorn*[18] in the light of this theory, we shall find countless examples of constantly generating melody emitting sparks of images which, in their brilliance, their sudden transitions, their headlong rush, reveal a power that is utterly alien to epic illusion and its peaceful flow. From the point of view of the epic this uneven and irregular world of images in lyric poetry is simply to be condemned: and certainly the solemn epic rhapsodies of Apolline festivals in the age of Terpander did just that.

In the poetry of the folk song, then, we see language doing its utmost *to imitate music*: hence, with Archilochus, we see the beginning of a new world of poetry that most profoundly contradicts the Homeric world. Thus we have described the only possible relationship between poetry and music, word and sound: now imbued with music's power, the word, the image and the concept seek an expression analogous to music. In this sense we can distinguish two main currents in the linguistic history of the Greek people, in which language imitated either the world of images and phenomena or the world of music. We need only consider the linguistic differences in colour, syntactical construction and phraseology in Homer and Pindar to understand the meaning of this opposition; it becomes immediately obvious that between

Homer and Pindar the *orgiastic flute melodies of Olympus* must have sounded – even in the age of Aristotle, in the midst of an infinitely more highly developed music, this music must have inspired a drunken enthusiasm, and certainly in its original effect have stirred the people of the day to imitate it with every available means of expression. I am here recalling a familiar phenomenon of our own time, one which is repellent to our aesthetic. Again and again, we hear individual listeners impelled by a Beethoven symphony to speak of it in images, even if any comparison of the various image worlds thus conjured up by a piece of music shows them to be fantastically diverse or even contradictory. Turning their feeble wits to such comparisons, and ignoring the phenomenon that truly demands explanation, is very much a part of that aesthetic. Indeed, even if the composer has discussed a composition in terms of images – if, for example, he has called a symphony 'Pastoral' and described one movement as 'Stream Scene', or another as 'Merry Gathering of Peasant Folk' – these are but symbols, ideas born from the music, and not the imitated objects of the music. They are ideas that have nothing to teach us about the *Dionysiac* content of the music, and have no distinctive value as images. We must now transfer this process of the discharge of music in images to a youthful people, fresh and linguistically creative, before we can have any idea of how the strophic folk song came about, and how the linguistic faculty as a whole was stimulated by the new principle of the imitation of music.

If we can therefore see lyric poetry as the imitative effulgence of music in images and concepts, we may now ask: 'How does music *appear* in the mirror of imagery and concepts?' *It appears as will* in Schopenhauer's sense of the word, as an opposite of the aesthetic, purely contemplative will-less state. We should here distinguish as sharply as possible between the concepts of essence and appearance: it is by its essence impossible for music to be will, since as such it would be entirely excluded from the realm of art, given that the will is precisely that which is not aesthetic; yet it is manifest as will. For in order to express its appearance in images, the lyric poet needs all the stirrings of passion, from the whisper of affection to the roar of madness; impelled to speak of music in

Apolline symbols, he sees the whole of nature, and himself within it, as eternally willing, desiring, yearning. But in so far as he interprets music in images, he himself lies amidst the peaceful waves of Apolline contemplation, though all that he considers through the medium of music may be in urgent, driven motion. Indeed, if he glimpses himself through the same medium, he sees his own image in the state of unappeased emotion: his own desire, his yearning, his moans and his jubilation become a symbol with which he interprets music to himself. This is the phenomenon of the lyric poet: as an Apolline genius he interprets music through the image of the will, while he himself, completely delivered of the greed of the will, is the pure and undimmed eye of the sun.

Throughout this discussion I have relied on the idea that lyric poetry is dependent on the spirit of music to the same extent as music itself, in its absolute sovereignty, does not *require* images or concepts but can *tolerate* both. Lyric poetry can express nothing that was not already most universally present, with the most universal validity, within the music that compelled the lyric poet to use the language of images. For this very reason, the world-symbolism of music cannot be exhaustively interpreted through language, because it symbolically refers to the primal contradiction and the primal suffering within the primal Oneness, and thus symbolizes a sphere beyond and prior to all phenomena. In comparison with this, all phenomena are mere symbols: hence *language*, as the organ and symbol of phenomena, can never uncover the innermost core of music but, once it attempts to imitate music, always remains in superficial contact with it, and no amount of lyrical eloquence can bring its deepest meaning a step closer.

7

We must now call upon all the aesthetic principles we have so far discussed in order to find our way around the labyrinth, which is how we must refer to the *origin of Greek tragedy*. I do not think I am making an extravagant claim when I say that the problem of this origin has not yet even been seriously tackled, however many times the tattered rags of the classical tradition have been sewn together in their various combinations, and ripped apart again. This tradition tell us quite categorically *that tragedy arose from the tragic chorus*, and was originally only chorus and nothing else. This is what obliges us to penetrate to the core of this tragic chorus as the true primal drama, disregarding the usual aesthetic clichés: that it is the ideal viewer, or that it represents the populace as against the noble realm of the drama proper. This latter interpretation, edifying as certain politicians may find it – suggesting that the immutable moral law of the democratic Athenians was represented in the popular chorus, always correct in its appraisal of the passionate misdeeds and extravagances of the kings – may indeed have been suggested by a phrase of Aristotle's: it can have had no influence on the original formation of tragedy, whose purely religious beginnings rule out the very idea of contrasting the populace with the nobility, as indeed they exclude the whole area of political and social concerns; but with reference to the classical form of the chorus as we know it from Aeschylus and Sophocles, we should also consider it blasphemous to speak of the idea of a presentiment of the 'constitutional representation of the people', though others have not shrunk from such sacrilege. Constitutional representation of the people was unknown to the classical polities, and it is to be hoped that the ancient tragedies had no such 'presentiment' of it.

Much more celebrated than this political explanation of the chorus is the idea put forward by A. W. Schlegel,[19] who proposes that we should see the chorus as being to some degree the epitome and concentration of the mass of spectators, the 'ideal spectator'. This view, when seen alongside the historically traditional idea that the tragedy was originally only the chorus, reveals itself in its true colours, a crude and unscientific yet brilliant statement, but one whose brilliance has been preserved only through the concentrated form of its expression, the truly Germanic predilection for everything that is called 'ideal', and our momentary astonishment. We will be truly astonished once we compare the theatre audience – one which we know very well – with that chorus, and ask ourselves whether it is indeed possible to idealize from that audience anything resembling the tragic chorus. We inwardly deny this, and are just as amazed by the boldness of Schlegel's claim as by the totally different nature of the German audience. We had actually always believed that the true spectator, whoever he might be, must always remain aware that he is watching a work of art and not an empirical reality, while the tragic chorus of the Greeks is required to grant the figures on the stage a physical existence. The chorus of the Oceanides really believes that it is seeing the Titan Prometheus, and thinks itself just as real as the stage god. And is that supposed to be the highest and purest kind of spectator, one who, like the Oceanides, believes that he sees Prometheus real and present in the flesh? And would it be a sign of the ideal spectator to run on to the stage and free the god from his tormentors? We had previously believed in an aesthetic audience, and seen the individual viewer as being all the more skilful the more capable he was of seeing the work of art as art, in an aesthetic way; and now Schlegel's pronouncement tells us that the perfect ideal viewer allows the world on stage to affect him not in an aesthetic way, but in a physically empirical way. 'Oh, those Greeks!' we sighed. 'They are turning our aesthetic on its head!' But once we had become accustomed to it, we repeated Schlegel's dictum every time the chorus was mentioned.

But the very emphatic tradition I mentioned before refutes Schlegel in this instance: the chorus as such, without the stage – the primitive form of tragedy, then – and the chorus of ideal spectators are incompatible. What sort of artistic genre would it be that took as its foundation the concept of the spectator, and whose actual form was 'the spectator as such'? The idea of the spectator without a play is an absurd one. I fear that the birth of tragedy may no more be explained with reference to respect for the moral intelligence of the masses than with reference to the concept of the spectator without a play, and I consider this problem too profound even to be touched on by such shallow interpretations.

An infinitely more valuable insight into the meaning of the chorus was put forward by Schiller in the famous preface to the *Bride of Messina*, in which he sees the chorus as a living wall that tragedy pulls around itself to close itself off entirely from the real world and maintain its ideal ground and its poetic freedom.

Schiller uses this as his chief weapon in his fight against the commonplace concept of naturalism, against the illusionism commonly demanded from dramatic poetry. While, for Schiller, in the theatre the daylight itself is merely artificial, the architecture is merely symbolic and the metrical language is idealized, delusions still predominate; it is not enough, for Schiller, that we should only tolerate as a poetic liberty what is in fact the essence of all poetry. The introduction of the chorus is the crucial step towards the open and honest declaration of war on all naturalism in art. This is the kind of interpretation, it seems to me, for which our own age, convinced of its superiority, uses the dismissive catchword 'pseudo-idealism'. I fear, on the other hand, that in our idolization of the natural and the real we have arrived at the opposite pole from our idealism – the realm of the wax museums. These too are without art, like certain popular novels of the present day: I only ask that I should not be troubled with the claim that in this art Schiller's and Goethe's 'pseudo-idealism' has been vanquished.

It is certainly the case, as Schiller rightly saw, that the ground walked upon by the Greek satyr chorus, the chorus of the original tragedy, is an 'ideal' ground, a ground lifted high above the real paths of mortal men. For this chorus the Greeks built the floating scaffold of an invented *natural state*, and placed upon it *natural beings* invented especially for it. It was on this foundation that tragedy arose, and it was indeed for this reason that it was excused from the start from precise depiction of reality. Yet this is not a world randomly imagined to fit in between heaven and earth; rather it is a world of equal reality and credibility, as Olympus with its inhabitants was for the Hellenes. The satyr, the Dionysiac chorist, lives in a world granted existence under the religious sanction of myth and ritual. That tragedy begins with him, that the Dionysiac wisdom of tragedy speaks through him, is for us a phenomenon just as surprising as the very origin of tragedy out of the chorus. Perhaps we shall find a point of departure for our reflections in the claim that the satyr, the invented natural being, relates to cultural humanity as Dionysiac music relates to civilization. Of the latter, Richard Wagner says that it is annulled by music as lamplight is annulled by the light of day. In the same way, I believe, the Greek man of culture felt himself annulled in the face of the satyr chorus, and the immediate effect of Dionysiac tragedy is that state and society, the gulfs separating man from man, make way for an overwhelming sense of unity that goes back to the very heart of nature. The metaphysical consolation (with which, as I wish to point out, every true tragedy leaves us), that whatever superficial changes may occur, life is at bottom indestructibly powerful and joyful, is given concrete form as a satyr chorus, a chorus of natural beings, living ineradicably behind all civilization, as it were, remaining the same for ever, regardless of the changing generations and the path of history.

This chorus was a consolation to the Hellene, thoughtful and uniquely susceptible as he was to the tenderest and deepest suffering, whose piercing gaze has seen to the core of the terrible destructions of world history and nature's cruelty; and who runs the risk of longing for a Buddha-like denial of the will. He is saved by art, and through art life has saved him for itself.

The ecstasy of the Dionysiac state, abolishing the habitual barriers and boundaries of existence, actually contains, for its duration, a lethargic element into which all past personal experience is plunged. Thus, through this gulf of oblivion, the worlds of everyday and Dionysiac reality become separated. But when one once more becomes aware of this everyday reality, it becomes repellent; this leads to a mood of asceticism, of denial of the will. This is something that Dionysiac man shares with Hamlet: both have truly seen to the essence of things, they have *understood*, and action repels them; for their action can change nothing in the eternal essence of things, they consider it ludicrous or shameful that they should be expected to restore order to the chaotic world. Understanding kills action, action depends on a veil of illusion – this is what Hamlet teaches us, not the stock interpretation of Hamlet as a John-a-dreams who, from too much reflection, from an excess of possibilities, so to speak, fails to act. Not reflection, not that! – True understanding, insight into the terrible truth, outweighs every motive for action, for Hamlet and Dionysiac man alike. No consolidation will be of any use from now on, longing passes over the world towards death, beyond the gods themselves; existence, radiantly reflected in the gods or in an immortal 'Beyond', is denied. Aware of truth from a single glimpse of it, all man can now see is the horror and absurdity of existence; now he understands the symbolism of Ophelia's fate, now he understands the wisdom of Silenus, the god of the woods: it repels him.

Here, in this supreme menace to the will, there approaches a redeeming, healing enchantress – *art*. She alone can turn these thoughts of repulsion at the horror and absurdity of existence into ideas compatible with life: these are the *sublime* – the taming of horror through art; and *comedy* – the artistic release from the repellence of the absurd. The satyr chorus of the dithyramb is the salvation of Greek art; the frenzies described above were exhausted in the middle world of these Dionysiac attendants.

8

The satyr, like the idyllic shepherd of our own more recent age, is the product of a longing for the primal and the natural; but how firmly and fearlessly did the Greeks hold on to this man of the woods, and how effeminately and timidly has modern man dallied with the flattering image of a dainty, flute-playing, sentimental shepherd! Nature, still unaffected by knowledge, the bolts of culture still unforced – that is what the Greeks saw in their satyr, and for that reason they did not conflate him with the apes. On the contrary – he was the archetype of man, the expression of his highest and most intense emotions, an inspired reveller enraptured by the closeness of his god, a sympathetic companion in whom god's suffering is repeated, the harbinger of wisdom from the very breast of nature, a symbol of nature's sexual omnipotence, which the Greeks were accustomed to considering with respectful astonishment. The satyr was something divine and sublime; he must have seemed particularly so to the painfully broken gaze of Dionysiac man. He would have been insulted by the dressed-up, meretricious shepherd: his eye rested in sublime satisfaction on the undisguised, untroubled and wondrous traits of nature; here, the illusion of culture had been erased from the archetype of man – it was here that the true man revealed himself, the bearded satyr celebrating his god. Before him, the man of culture shrivelled up into a mendacious caricature. Schiller was right in his appraisal of these origins of tragic art: the chorus is a living wall against encroaching reality because it – the satyr chorus – depicts existence more truly, more authentically, more completely than the man of culture who sees himself as the sole reality. The realm of poetry does not lie outside the world, a fantastic impossibility, the product of a poet's mind; it wishes to be precisely the opposite of this, the unadorned expression of truth, and must for that very reason cast off the mendacious finery of the supposed reality of the man of culture. The contrast between this authentic, natural truth and the lie of culture masquerading as the sole reality is like the contrast between the eternal core of things, the thing in itself, and the entire world of phenomena; and just as tragedy, with its metaphysical consolation, points to the eternal life of that core and the constant destruction of phenomena, the symbolism of the satyr chorus analogously expresses the primal relationship between the thing in itself and the world of appearances. Modern man's idyllic shepherd is nothing but a counterfeit of the sum of cultural illusions that he takes to be nature; the Dionysiac Greek wanted truth and nature at the summit of their power – and saw himself transformed into a satyr.

The ecstatic horde of Dionysiac votaries celebrated under the influence of such moods and insights, whose power was so transformed before their very eyes that they imagined they saw themselves as reconstituted geniuses of nature, as satyrs. The later constitution of the tragic chorus is the artistic imitation of this natural phenomenon, which required a separation between Dionysiac spectators and Dionysiac votaries who are under the god's spell. But we must never forget that the audience of the Attic tragedy discovered itself in the chorus of the orchestra, and that there was no fundamental opposition between the audience and the chorus: for everything was simply a great, sublime chorus of dancing, singing satyrs, or of those whom the satyrs represented. Schlegel's phrase must take on a different sense in this context. The chorus is the 'ideal spectator' in so far as it is the only *viewer*, the viewer of the visionary world on the stage. The audience of spectators as we know it was unknown to the Greeks: in their theatres anyone in the terraces, rising in concentric arcs, was able to *overlook* the whole of the surrounding cultural world, and, in satisfied contemplation, to imagine themselves members of the chorus. Thus we may call the chorus, at this primitive stage of the original tragedy, a reflection of Dionysiac man for his own contemplation. We can imagine this phenomenon most clearly if we think of an actor who, such is his talent, can see the role that he is to perform hovering palpably before his eyes. The satyr chorus is primarily a vision of the Dionysiac mass, just as the world on the stage is a vision of this satyr chorus: the power of this vision is strong enough to make the gaze dull and unresponsive to the impression of 'reality', to the men of culture in the seats all around. The shape of the Greek theatre recalls a lonely mountain valley: the stage architecture appears as a luminous cloud formation seen by the Bacchae, as they swarm down from the mountains, as the wonderful frame in the middle of which the image of Dionysus is revealed to them.

To our scholarly view of the elemental artistic processes, this primal aesthetic phenomenon, evoked as a way of explaining the tragic chorus, is almost repellent; while nothing could be clearer than that the poet becomes a poet only by seeing himself surrounded by characters living and acting before him, and allowing him to see into their innermost natures. A particularly modern weakness inclines us to see the primal aesthetic phenomenon in too complicated and abstract a way. For the true poet the metaphor is not a rhetorical figure but a representative image that really hovers before him in place of a concept. For him, the character is not a whole laboriously assembled from individual traits, but a person, insistently living before his eyes, distinguished from the otherwise identical vision of the painter by his continuous life and action. How is it that Homer describes things so much more visually than any other poet? Because he looks so much more clearly. We talk of poetry in such an abstract way because most of us are bad poets. The aesthetic phenomenon is fundamentally a simple one: grant someone only the ability continually to see a living play, to live constantly surrounded by hordes of spirits, and he will be a poet. If one feels the desire to transform oneself and to speak from other bodies and souls, one is a dramatist.

Dionysiac excitement is capable of communicating to a whole crowd of people the artistic gift of seeing itself surrounded by a host of spirits with which it knows itself to be profoundly united. This process is the primal dramatic phenomenon in the tragic chorus: seeing oneself transformed and acting as though one had truly entered another body, another character. This process is the start of the evolution of the drama. This is a different matter from the rhapsodist who does not fuse with his images but rather, like the painter, sees them outside himself with a contemplative eye; it is an abandonment of individuality by entering another character. And this phenomenon appears with epidemic frequency: a whole host of people can be cast under this spell. For this reason the dithyramb is significantly different from all other forms of choric song. The virgins who solemnly enter the temple of Apollo, laurel branches in their hands, singing a processional song, remain who they are and keep their names as citizens: the dithyrambic chorus is a chorus of people transformed, whose civic past and social status are completely forgotten: they have become the timeless worshippers of their god, beyond all social contingencies. All the other choral lyrics of the Greeks are merely a tremendous intensification of the individual Apolline singer, while in the dithyramb a community of unconscious actors stands before us, seeing themselves as transformed.

Enchantment is the precondition of all dramatic art. In this enchantment the Dionysiac reveller sees himself as a satyr, *and it is as a satyr that he looks upon the god*: in his transformation he sees a new vision outside himself, the Apolline complement of his state. With this new vision the drama is complete.

In the light of this insight, we must see Greek tragedy as the Dionysiac chorus, continuously discharging itself in an Apolline world of images. Those choric sections which recur throughout the tragedy are therefore, so to speak, the womb of what is called the dialogue, the entire on-stage world, the drama proper. In several successive discharges this primal ground of tragedy radiates that vision of the drama which is entirely a dream phenomenon and thus epic in nature, but on the other hand, as the objectification of a Dionysiac state, it is not Apolline redemption through illusion but rather a representation of the fragmentation of the individual and his unification with primal being. Thus the drama is the Apolline symbol of Dionysiac knowledge and Dionysiac effects, and consequently separated from the epic as by a tremendous chasm.

This interpretation perfectly explains the *chorus* in Greek tragedy, the symbol of the crowd in a Dionysiac state. Accustomed as we are to the function of a chorus on the modern stage, and the operatic chorus in particular, we are unable to understand that the tragic chorus of the Greeks is older, more primordial, indeed more important than the 'action' itself – as tradition has so clearly told us. Given that traditionally great importance and originality, we cannot discern why it should have been made up exclusively of humble votaries, at first only of goat-like satyrs, and the orchestra in front of the stage was always a puzzle to us. But we now know that the stage, and the action, were fundamentally and originally conceived only as a *vision*, that the sole 'reality' is the chorus, which generates the vision from within itself, and speaks of it with all the symbolism of dance, sound and words. In its vision this chorus beholds its lord and master, Dionysus, and hence it is always a chorus of *votaries*: it sees how he, the god, suffers and is exalted, and it therefore does not *act* itself. In this function of complete devotion to the god, it is the supreme, Dionysiac expression of *nature*, and therefore, like nature, it speaks under the spell of wise and oracular sayings. *Sharing his suffering*, it is also *wise*, heralding the truth from the very heart of the world. This is the origin of that fantastic, apparently repellent figure of the wise and inspired satyr, which is also the 'simple man' in contrast to the god: the image of nature and nature's strongest impulses, the symbol of those impulses and also the herald of its wisdom and art – musician, poet, dancer and clairvoyant in a single person.

At first *Dionysus*, the true stage hero and the focus of the vision, is, in the light of this insight and according to tradition, not really present in the very oldest period of tragedy, but is only imagined to be present: tragedy, that is, is originally 'chorus' and not 'drama'. Later, the attempt is made to show the god as real, and to represent the visionary form as well as its transfiguring frame in a form visible to all eyes: this is the beginning of the 'drama' in the narrower sense. Now the dithyrambic chorus is given the task of stimulating the mood of the audience in such a Dionysiac way that when the tragic hero appears on the stage they do not see, for example, the awkwardly masked man, but rather a visionary form born, so to speak, out of their own rapt vision. If we consider Admetus lost in contemplation, recalling his recently departed wife Alcestis and completely consumed by his imaginary vision of her – and suddenly a woman with a similar form and gait is led towards him in disguise; if we imagine his sudden tremor of unease, his impetuous comparison, his instinctive conviction – then we have an analogy to the emotion that the spectator felt when, in a state of Dionysiac excitement, he saw the god, with whose suffering he had already identified, walking on to the stage. He involuntarily translated the entire image of the god that was trembling before his soul to that masked figure, and dissolved its reality into a ghostly unreality. This is the Apolline dream state, in which the daylight world is veiled and a new world, more distinct, comprehensible and affecting than the other and yet more shadowy, is constantly reborn before our eyes. Accordingly, we can see a radical contrast of styles in tragedy: the language, colour, mobility and dynamic of speech become completely separate spheres of expression in the Dionysiac lyric of the chorus and the Apolline dream world of the stage. The Apolline phenomena in which Dionysus is objectified are no longer 'a boundless sea, a changing weft, a glowing life', like the music of the chorus; they are not only those powers that the inspired worshipper of Dionysus merely feels and does not condense into an image, in which he feels the closeness of the god. Now, the clarity and solidity of the epic form speak to him from the stage. Dionysus no longer speaks through powers, but as an epic hero, almost with the language of Homer.

9

Everything that comes to the surface in the Apolline part of Greek tragedy, the dialogue, looks simple, transparent and beautiful. In this sense the dialogue is an image of the Hellene, whose nature is revealed in dance, because in dance the greatest strength is only potential, but is betrayed in the suppleness and luxuriance of movement. Thus the language of Sophoclean heroes surprises us with its Apolline precision and lucidity, so that we immediately imagine we can see into the innermost core of their being, somewhat astonished that the way to that core is such a short one. But if we leave aside the characteristics of the hero – who is basically merely a light-image cast on a dark screen, *appearance* through and through – that come to the surface and attain visibility; if we instead penetrate the myth projected in these bright reflections, we suddenly experience something that is the opposite of a familiar optical phenomenon. If we make a concerted effort to stare into the sun and turn away blinded, we have dark-coloured patches before our eyes as what we might call remedies. The light-image manifestations of the Sophoclean hero – the Apolline mask, in short – are the inevitable products of a glance into the terrible depths of nature: light-patches, we might say, to heal the gaze seared by terrible night. Only in this sense can we imagine that we correctly understand the serious and meaningful concept of 'Greek cheerfulness' – while today, of course, we constantly encounter this concept of cheerfulness wrongly understood as a state of untroubled contentment.

Sophocles saw the most suffering character on the Greek stage, the unhappy Oedipus, as the noble man who is predestined for error and misery despite his wisdom, but who finally, through his terrible suffering, exerts a magical and beneficial power that continues to prevail after his death. The noble man does not sin, the profound poet wishes to tell us: through his actions every law, every natural order, the whole moral world can be destroyed, and through these actions a higher magic circle of effects is drawn, founding a new world on the ruins of the old, now destroyed. This is what the poet, in so far as he is also a religious thinker, wishes to say to us: as a poet, he first presents us with a wonderfully intricate legal knot which the judge slowly unravels, piece by piece, to his own ruin; such is the truly Hellenic delight in this dialectical unravelment that it casts a sense of triumphant cheerfulness over the whole work, and takes the sting from all the terrible premises of the plot. In *Oedipus at Colonus* we encounter this same cheerfulness, but elevated in a process of infinite transfiguration. The aged man, afflicted by an excess of misery, abandoned to every misfortune that comes his way as a passively *suffering* man, is confronted by a superterrestrial cheerfulness that descends from the gods, which suggests to us that the hero, through his passivity, has found his supreme activity, the effects of which will resonate far beyond his own life, while his conscious strivings in his former life led him only to passivity. Thus the legal knot of the Oedipus fable, which mortal eyes could not disentangle, is slowly unravelled – and the most profound human delight overcomes us at the sight of this divine counterpart of the dialectic.

If this explanation does justice to the poet, we may still ask whether it has exhausted the content of the myth: and here it becomes apparent that the whole vision of the poet is nothing but that light-image that healing nature holds up to us after we have glimpsed the abyss. Oedipus his father's murderer, his mother's husband, Oedipus who solved the riddle of the Sphinx! What can we learn from the cryptic trinity of these fateful deeds? There is an ancient folk belief, particularly prevalent in Persia, that a wise magus can be born only from incest: our immediate interpretation of this, with reference to Oedipus the riddle-solver and suitor of his own mother, is that for clairvoyant and magical powers to have broken the spell of the present and the future, the rigid law of individuation and the true magic of nature itself, the cause must have been a monstrous crime against nature – incest in this case; for how could nature be forced to offer up her secrets if not by being triumphantly resisted – by unnatural acts? I see this insight as quite clearly present in the terrible trinity that shapes Oedipus' fate: the man who solves the riddle of nature – of the dual-natured Sphinx – must also, as his father's murderer and his mother's lover, transgress the sacred codes of nature. Indeed, what the myth seems to whisper to us is that wisdom, and Dionysiac wisdom in particular, is an abominable crime against nature; that anyone who, through his knowledge, casts nature into the abyss of destruction, must himself experience the dissolution of nature.

'The blade of wisdom is turned against the wise; wisdom is a crime against nature': such are the awful sentences that the myth cries out to us. But like a beam of sunlight the Hellenic poet touches the sublime and terrible Memnon's Column of the myth, which suddenly begins to resound in Sophoclean melodies!

I shall now contrast the glory of passivity with the glory of activity that illuminates Aeschylus' *Prometheus*. What the thinker Aeschylus had to say, but what as a poet he only hinted at with his symbolic image, the young Goethe revealed in the bold words of his Prometheus:

Hier sitz' ich, forme Menschen
Nach meinem Bilde,
Ein Geschlecht, das mir gleich sei,
Zu leiden, zu weinen,
Zu genießen und zu freuen sich,
Und dein nicht zu achten,
Wie ich!

(Here I sit, making men
In my image,
A race which shall be like me,
To suffer, to weep,
To enjoy and be glad,
And to ignore you,
As I do!)

Man, rising to Titanic stature, fights for his own culture and compels allegiance from the gods, because in his very own wisdom he has their existence and their limitations under his command. But the most wonderful thing about the Prometheus poem, which is, by virtue of its fundamental idea, a true hymn of impiety, is its profound Aeschylean longing for *justice*: the immeasurable suffering of the bold 'individual' on the one hand and the divine tribulation, the intimation of a twilight of the gods, on the other; the power of both suffering worlds compelling reconciliation, metaphysical unity, insistently recalls the core and the chief premise of Aeschylus' view of the world, which sees the Moira enthroned as eternal justice above gods and men. Given the astounding boldness with which Aeschylus places the Olympian world on his scales of justice, we must not forget that the profound Greek had an unshakeable substratum of metaphysical thought in his mysteries, and was able to discharge all his feelings of scepticism on to the Olympian gods. The Greek artist in particular felt an obscure sense of reciprocal dependency with these gods – and this feeling is symbolized in the Prometheus of Aeschylus. The Titanic artist found within himself the defiant belief that he was enabled to create men and at least to destroy Olympian gods by his superior wisdom, for which he was, of course, compelled to atone with eternal suffering. The glorious 'ability' of the great genius, for which even eternal suffering is not recompense enough, the austere pride of the *artist*, is the very essence of Aeschylean poetry, while in his *Oedipus* Sophocles intones, as a prelude, song of triumph to the *saint*.

But even Aeschylus' interpretation of the myth does not plumb the full depths of its terrors: the artist's desire for development, the cheerfulness of artistic creation in its defiance of all misfortune, is merely a bright image of clouds and sky reflected on a black lake of sorrow. The story of Prometheus is the indigenous property of all Aryan peoples, and a testament to their talent for profundity and tragedy – indeed it may well be that this myth has precisely the same characteristic meaning for the Aryan spirit as does the myth of the Fall for the Semitic, and that the two myths are as siblings to one another. But the premise for the Prometheus myth is the supreme value that primitive man places on *fire* as the true palladium of any rising culture: but the idea that man has complete control of fire, and does not only receive it as a gift from heaven, as a kindling bolt of lightning or a warming sunbeam, struck those contemplative primitive men as a sacrilege, a plundering of divine nature. And thus the first philosophical problem created a painful and insoluble contradiction between man and the gods, and placed it like a boulder at the gates of every culture. The best and highest blessing that mankind can attain was won by an act of sacrilege, and man must now take the consequences – the tide of suffering and troubles with which the offended divinities punish the nobly ambitious human race: a severe idea, which by the *dignity* that it confers on sacrilege contrasts oddly with the Semitic myth of the

Fall, in which curiosity, mendacious deception, susceptibility, lasciviousness – a whole series of predominantly feminine attributes – were seen as the origin of evil. What distinguishes the Aryan version is the sublime idea of *active sin* as the truly Promethean virtue: this provides both the ethical background to pessimistic tragedy and the justification of human evil, and hence of human guilt as well as the suffering it brings. Misfortune the essence of things – which the contemplative Aryan was not inclined to quibble away – the contradiction at the heart of the world was revealed to him as a confusion of different worlds, a divine and a human world, for example, both individually in the right, but each merely one individual beside another, suffering from its individuation. In the individual's heroic effort to achieve universality, in the attempt to escape the spell of individuation, to become the only being in the world, he encounters the hidden primal contradiction – he commits sacrilege, that is, and he suffers. Thus the Aryans saw sacrilege as a man, while the Semites saw sin as a woman, just as the primal sacrilege was committed by man, the primal sin by woman. As the witches' chorus has it, incidentally:

> Wir nehmen das nicht so genau:
> Mit tausend Schritten macht's die Frau;
> Doch wie sie auch sich eilen kann,
> Mit einem Sprunge macht's der Mann.[20]
>
> (That's not exactly what we'd say:
> A thousand steps is woman's way;
> But however fast she covers ground
> Man does it in a single bound.)

Once we understand the innermost core of the Prometheus myth – the necessity of sacrilege that confronts the Titanically striving individual – we must also immediately perceive the non-Apolline qualities of this pessimistic idea. For Apollo seeks to pacify individuals by drawing boundaries between them, and by repeatedly calling them to mind as the most sacred universal laws in his demands for self-knowledge and moderation. But lest the Apolline tendency should freeze all form into an Egyptian rigidity and coldness, lest the effort to prescribe the course and compass of the individual wave should still the motion of the lake, from time to time the Dionysiac flood-tide destroyed all the little circles with which the one-sided Apolline 'will' sought to captivate Hellenism. The sudden rise of the Dionysiac tide then takes upon its back the little individual wavelets, just as Prometheus' brother, the Titan Atlas, took the world on his. This Titanic impulse to become the Atlas of all individuals, and on one's broad back to bear them ever higher, ever further, is the bond that unites the Promethean and the Dionysiac. In this respect the Aeschylean Prometheus is a Dionysiac mask, while in the profound longing for justice that I have already mentioned, Aeschylus reveals his paternal descent from Apollo, the god of individuation and of just boundaries, the god of understanding. And the two-faced nature of the Aeschylean Prometheus, at once Apolline and Promethean, might be expressed in this conceptual formula: 'All that exists is just and unjust and equally justified in both.'

Your world, this! So that's a world![21]

10

It is an uncontested tradition that Greek tragedy in its oldest form dealt only with the sufferings of Dionysus, and that for a long time Dionysus was the only theatrical hero. But we may claim with equal certainty that, until Euripides, Dionysus never ceased to be the tragic hero, and that all the celebrated characters of the Greek stage – Prometheus, Oedipus and so on – are merely masks of that original hero, Dionysus. The fact that a divinity lurks behind all these masks is the major reason for the typical 'ideality' of those celebrated characters that has so often aroused astonishment. Someone, I do not know who, claims that all individuals, as individuals, are comic and consequently untragic: from which we can deduce that the Greeks were actually *unable* to bear individuals on the tragic stage. And they do seem to have felt that way, just as the Platonic distinguishing valuation of the 'idea' as against the 'idol' lies deep within the Hellenic spirit. But to use Plato's terminology, we might speak of the tragic figures of the Hellenic stage rather as follows: the one real Dionysus appears in a multiplicity of figures, in the mask of a warrior hero and, we might say, entangled in the net of the individual will. As the god on stage speaks and acts, he resembles an erring, striving, suffering individual: and the fact that he *appears* with this precision and clarity is the effect of Apollo, the interpreter of dreams, who shows the chorus its Dionysiac state through this symbolic appearance. In fact, however, this hero is the suffering Dionysus of the mysteries, the god who himself experiences the suffering of individuation, of whom marvellous myths relate that he was dismembered by the Titans and that, in this condition, he is worshipped as Zagreus. This suggests that dismemberment, the true Dionysiac *suffering*, amounts to a transformation into air, water, earth and fire, and that we should therefore see the condition of individuation as the source and origin of all suffering and hence as something reprehensible. From the smile of this Dionysus were born the Olympian gods, from his tears mankind. In his existence as a dismembered god Dionysus had the dual nature of a cruel, savage daemon and a mild, gentle ruler. But the hope of the epopts was the rebirth of Dionysus, which we can now interpret, with some foreboding, as the end of individuation: the roaring hymn of joy of the epopts celebrated the coming of this third Dionysus. This hope alone casts a ray of joy across the face of the world, torn and fragmented into individuals, mythically symbolized by Demeter, sunk in eternal grief, who *rejoices* once more only when told that she can give birth to Dionysus *again*. In these ideas we already have all the component parts of a profound and pessimistic view of the world, and at the same time the *mystery doctrine of tragedy*: the basic understanding of the unity of all things, individuation seen as the primal source of evil, art as the joyful hope that the spell of individuation can be broken, as a presentiment of a restored oneness.

We suggested earlier that the Homeric epic is the poetry of Olympian culture, its own song of triumph about the terrors of the battle with the Titans. Now, under the overwhelming influence of tragic poetry, the Homeric myths are reborn in a different form, and in this metempsychosis show that Olympian culture too has been vanquished by an even deeper vision of the world. The defiant Titan Prometheus informed his Olympian tormentor that his supremacy was in the greatest danger if he delayed too long in joining forces with him. In Aeschylus we see Zeus, terrified and fearful of his end, forging an alliance with the Titan. Thus the former age of the Titans is belatedly brought back from Tartarus into the light of day. The philosophy of wild and naked nature sees the myths of the Homeric world dancing by, with the frank and honest gaze of truth: they blanch, they tremble under the flashing eye of this goddess – until the mighty fist of the Dionysiac artist compels them to worship this new deity. Dionysiac truth takes over the whole sphere of myth as a symbolic expression of its own insights, and gives it voice partly in the public cult of tragedy and partly in the secret rites of the dramatic mysteries, but always in the old mythic trappings. What was this force that freed Prometheus from his vultures and made myth the vehicle of Dionysiac wisdom? It was the Herculean force of music – which, supremely manifested in tragedy, was able to interpret myth with a new and most profound eloquence. This, as we have already shown, is music's most powerful capacity. For it is the lot of all myths to creep gradually into the confines of a supposedly historical reality, and to be treated by some later age as unique fact with claims to historical truth; and the Greeks, cleverly and capriciously, were already well on the way to recasting the whole of their youthful mythic dream as a pragmatic *youthful history*. For this is how religions tend to die: the mythic premises of a religion are systematized, beneath the stern and intelligent eyes of an orthodox dogmatism, into a fixed sum of historical events; one begins nervously defending the veracity of myths, at the same time resisting their continuing life and growth. The feeling for myth dies and is replaced by religious claims to foundations in history. This dying myth was now seized by the new-born genius of Dionysiac music; and in the hand of that music it blossomed anew, with colours such as it had never shown before, with a fragrance that hinted wistfully at the existence of a metaphysical world. After this last florescence it decays, its leaves wither, and soon the mocking Lucians of antiquity are clutching at the faded, ravaged blossoms as they are carried away by the four winds. It is through tragedy that myth attains its most profound content, its most expressive form; it rises up once more, like a wounded hero, and all the surplus energy, together with the sagacious calm of the dying man, burns in its eyes with a last, powerful glow.

What was your wish, sacrilegious Euripides, when you tried to force that dying myth into your service once more?[22] It died beneath your violent hands: and then you needed a counterfeit, masked myth which, like Heracles' monkey, could only deck itself out in the old finery. And as myth died for you, so the genius of music died as well: though you greedily plundered all the gardens of music, all you could manage was a counterfeit, masked music. And because you abandoned Dionysus, Apollo in his turn abandoned you; though you rouse all the passions from their beds and bewitch them into your circle, though you whet and hone a sophistical dialectic for the speeches of your heroes, they too will have only counterfeit, masked passions, and speak only counterfeit, masked speeches.

11

Greek tragedy met her death in a different way from all the older sister arts: she died tragically by her own hand, after irresolvable conflicts, while the others died happy and peaceful at an advanced age. If a painless death, leaving behind beautiful progeny, is the sign of a happy natural state, then the endings of the other arts show us the example of just such a happy natural state: they sink slowly, and with their dying eyes they behold their fairer offspring, who lift up their heads in bold impatience. The death of Greek tragedy, on the other hand, left a great void whose effects were felt profoundly, far and wide; as once Greek sailors in Tiberius' time heard the distressing cry 'the god Pan is dead' issuing from a lonely island, now, throughout the Hellenic world, this cry resounded like an agonized lament: 'Tragedy is dead! Poetry itself died with it! Away, away with you, puny, stunted imitators! Away with you to Hades, and eat your fill of the old masters' crumbs!'

But when a new artistic genre did spring into life, honouring tragedy as its predecessor and its master, it was frighteningly apparent that although it bore its mother's features they were the features she had borne during her long death-struggle. It was *Euripides* who fought tragedy's death-struggle; the later genre is known as the *New Attic Comedy*. It was in comedy that the degenerate figure of tragedy lived on, a monument to its miserable and violent death.

This context enables us to understand the passionate affection in which the poets of the New Comedy held Euripides; so that we are no longer startled by the desire of Philemon, who wished to be hanged at once so that he might meet Euripides in the underworld, as long as he could be sure that the deceased was still in full possession of his senses. But if we wished, quite briefly and without claiming to be exhaustive, to identify the bonds that linked Euripides with Menander and Philemon, and to say what they found exciting and exemplary in him, we need say only that Euripides brought the *spectator* on to the stage. Once we have recognized the stuff of which the pre-Euripidean Promethean dramatists shaped their heroes, and understood how little concerned they were to bring on to the stage an accurate mask of reality, we shall also understand the quite opposite tendency in Euripides. Through him, everyday man pushed his way through the auditorium on to the stage, and the mirror in which only great and bold features had hitherto found expression now showed the painful fidelity that also reflected the blemished lines of nature. Odysseus, the typical Hellene of the older art, now sank, beneath the hands of the new poets, into the figure of the Graeculus, who from this point onwards occupied centre-stage as a good-natured, cunning slave. What Euripides, in the *Frogs* of Aristophanes, accounts a merit in himself – that he has, with his nostrum, rid tragic art of its pompous obesity – is particularly apparent in his tragic heroes. In essence, the spectator now saw and heard his double on the Euripidean stage, and was overjoyed by his eloquence. But joy was not all: Euripides taught the people to speak for themselves, as he boasts in his competition with Aeschylus – how he taught the people to observe, to act and to think logically, artfully and with the cleverest sophistries. In this transformation of ordinary language he paved the way for the new comedy. For from that point on, it was no longer a mystery how to represent everyday life on the stage, and which maxims to use. The bourgeois mediocrity on which Euripides staked all his political hopes now had its chance to speak, where previously its dramatic language had been defined in tragedy by the demigod, and in comedy by the drunken satyr, the half-human. And Aristophanes' Euripides was able to pride himself on having portrayed mundane, commonplace, everyday life, which anyone was in a position to judge. If the populace was now philosophizing, conducting its business and pleading its legal cases with a hitherto unknown shrewdness, this was his doing, the product of the wisdom he had inculcated in the people.

It was to such a primed and enlightened populace that the new comedy was now able to address itself, with Euripides as a kind of chorus-master – although this time the chorus of spectators needed some rehearsing. Once this chorus was practised at singing in the Euripidean key, there came to the fore the dramatic genre that is like a game of chess, the New Comedy, with its perpetual triumphs of cunning and guile. But Euripides – the chorus-master – was the object of untiring praise: indeed, there were some who would have killed themselves to learn more from him, had they not known that the tragic poet was just as dead as tragedy itself. But along with tragedy the Hellene had relinquished belief in his immortality, belief not only in an ideal past, but also in an ideal future. The celebrated epitaph, 'frivolous and whimsical in old age', applies equally well to the senescent phase of Hellenism. The pleasure of the moment, wit, whimsy and caprice were its supreme deities; the fifth estate, the slaves, now came into its own, at least in attitude: and if we may still speak at all of 'Greek cheerfulness', we mean the cheerfulness of the slave, who has no serious responsibilities and nothing great to strive for, and who values nothing, past or future, more highly than the present. It was this illusion of 'Greek cheerfulness' that so enraged the profound and formidable minds of the first four centuries after Christ: they considered this womanish flight from seriousness and terror, this craven acquiescence in cosy enjoyment, not only contemptible but the very opposite of the Christian attitude. And it is due to their influence that the vision of Greek antiquity that survived for centuries, with almost unconquerable resilience, retained the rosy hues of cheerfulness – as though there had never been a sixth century, with its birth of tragedy, its mysteries, its Pythagoras and Heraclitus; as though the works of art from that great age simply did not exist. Yet none of those works could have grown from the soil of such a senescent, slavish cheerfulness and pleasure in life, and they point to a completely different vision of the world as the basis for their existence.

In asserting as I have done that Euripides brought the spectator on to the stage in order to render the spectator competent to judge the drama, I may have given the impression that the older tragic art had always had a poor relationship with the spectator; and one might be tempted to praise Euripides' radical intentions, aiming for an appropriate relationship between the work and the audience, as marking an advance over the work of Sophocles. But 'audience' is merely a word, and not a constant, immutable standard. Why should the artist feel obliged to accommodate himself to a force whose strength lies purely in its numbers? And if he feels superior, in talent and aspiration, to every single spectator, how could he feel greater respect for the collective expression of all those subordinate capacities than for that individual spectator who is, in relative terms, the most gifted among them? In truth, no Greek artist treated his audience with greater audacity and self-sufficiency throughout a whole lifetime than did Euripides: he who, even when the populace threw itself at his feet, publicly and with sublime defiance renounced his own intentions, those same intentions that had established his victory over the populace. Had this genius had the slightest reverence for the pandemonium that was his audience, he would have collapsed beneath the bludgeons of his failures long before the mid-course of his life. We now come to realize that our formula: 'Euripides brought the spectator on to the stage to render the spectator capable of judgement', was merely provisional, and that we must look further for a deeper understanding of his intentions. On the other hand, everyone knows that Aeschylus and Sophocles were held in the highest popular favour in their lifetimes and long afterwards, so we cannot speak of poor relationships between the work and the audience. What was it that drove the richly talented, tirelessly creative artist so violently away from a path illumined by the sun of the greatest poets and the clear sky of popular favour? What strange consideration for the spectator led him towards the spectator? How did an excessive respect for his audience lead him to treat his audience with disrespect?

As a poet, Euripides felt – and this is the answer to the riddle that we have just expressed – superior to the populace, but not to two of his spectators: he brought the populace on to the stage, but revered those two spectators as the sole judges and masters competent to judge his art as a whole; following their directives and exhortations he translated the whole world of emotions, passions and experiences, hitherto present in the ranks of spectators, into the souls of his stage heroes, deferring to them in his quest for a new language, a new music for these new characters. In their voices alone he heard both conclusive verdicts on his work and the encouragement that promised victory when the judgement of the audience once more held him in disfavour.

One of these two spectators is Euripides himself: Euripides the *thinker*, not the poet. It might be said that the extraordinary richness of his critical talent, like that of Lessing, while it might not have generated a supplementary productive impetus to his art, at least gave it constant sustenance. With this talent, this critical brilliance and agility, Euripides had sat in the theatre striving to rediscover in the masterworks of his great predecessors feature after feature, line after line, which time had darkened as it darkens old paintings. And in doing so he had discovered what anyone initiated into the deep secrets of Aeschylean tragedy might have expected: in every feature, every line, he found something incommensurable, a certain deceptive precision and at the same time an enigmatic depth, an infinite background. The clearest character still had a comet's tail attached to it, which seemed to point to uncertainty, to something that could not be illuminated. The same twilight shrouded the structure of the play, particularly the meaning of the chorus. And how dubious the solution of the ethical problems remained to him! How questionable the treatment of myth! How irregular the distribution of fortune and misfortune! Even in the language of the older tragedies he found much that was repellent, or puzzling at the very least. In particular, he found too much pomp for simple relationships, too many tropes and monstrosities for such plain characters. He sat there in the theatre, brooding restlessly, and he, as a spectator, confessed that he did not understand his great predecessors. But given his belief that reason was the true source of all enjoyment and creativity, he was obliged to wonder whether no one else thought as he did and admitted the existence of this incommensurability. But the multitude, and its finest individuals, answered him only with a suspicious smile; yet no one could tell him why, despite his doubts and misgivings, the great masters were right. And in this tormented state he came upon *the second spectator*, who did not understand tragedy and therefore chose to ignore it. Having joined forces with him, he was able, from his isolated position, to launch his tremendous battle against the works of Aeschylus and Sophocles – not by means of polemics, but as a dramatic poet, confronting traditional conceptions of tragedy with his own.

12

Before we give a name to this second spectator, let us cast our minds back for a moment to the description of the contradictory and incommensurable elements of Aeschylean tragedy. Let us remember our own surprise at the *chorus* and the *tragic hero* in that form of tragedy, which we could not reconcile either with our own habits or with tradition, until we recognized that this duality was the very origin and essence of Greek tragedy, the expression of two interwoven artistic impulses, *the Apolline and the Dionysiac.*

The excision of the primitive and powerful Dionysiac element from tragedy, and the rebuilding of tragedy on non-Dionysiac art, morality and philosophy – this is the intention of Euripides, now revealed to us as clear as day.

At the end of his life Euripides himself emphatically confronted his contemporaries with the question of the value and significance of this intention in a myth. Can the Dionysiac exist at all? Can it not be forcibly eradicated from Hellenic soil? Certainly, says the poet, if only such a thing were possible – but the god Dionysus is too powerful: the most intelligent adversary, like Pentheus in the *Bacchae*, is unwittingly bewitched by him, and in his enchantment runs headlong to his doom. The judgement of the two aged men, Cadmus and Tiresias, seems to be the judgement of the aged poet as well: the reasoning of the cleverest individual cannot overthrow those ancient popular traditions, that perpetually repropagated worship of Dionysus – indeed it is proper at least to make a show of cautious and diplomatic interest to such marvellous powers, although the god may well take offence at such a tepid degree of involvement and finally turn the diplomat – in this case Cadmus – into a dragon. This is the message of a poet who has heroically resisted Dionysus throughout his whole life, only to end his career by glorifying his opponent and committing suicide like a man hurling himself from a tower in order to escape the terrible, unbearable dizziness of vertigo. This tragedy is a protest against the fulfilment of his intentions – and oh, they had already been fulfilled! The miracle had occurred: by the time the poet recanted, his intentions had already emerged triumphant. Dionysus had already been hounded from the stage by a daemonic power that spoke through Euripides. Euripides too was, in a particular sense, merely a mask: the deity that spoke through him was not Dionysus, nor yet Apollo, but a new-born daemon bearing the name of *Socrates*. That was the new opposition: the Dionysiac and the Socratic, and that conflict was to be the downfall of Greek tragedy. Although Euripides might try to console us with his recantation, he could not do so: the most magnificent temple lay in ruins; what use were the lamentations of its destroyer, his admission that this had been the most beautiful of all temples? Or even that all subsequent critics have, as a punishment, turned him into a dragon – who could be satisfied by this pitiful compensation?

Let us now turn to the *Socratic* intention, with which Euripides fought and vanquished Aeschylean tragedy.

We must now ask ourselves what, given the most ideal circumstances, could have been the aim of the Euripidean intention of basing tragedy solely on non-Dionysiac precepts? What form of tragedy would we be left with if it were born from the womb of music, in the mysterious Dionysiac twilight? Nothing but *a dramatized epic*: an Apolline sphere of art in which *tragic* effects were impossible. This does not depend on the content of the events portrayed – indeed I would assert that in his projected *Nausicaa* Goethe could not have made the suicide of that idyllic being, which was to occupy the fifth act, tragically gripping. So tremendous is the power of the Apolline epic that it enchants the most terrible events before us with delight in illusion and in redemption through illusion. The poet of the dramatized epic can no more merge completely with his images than can the epic rhapsodist. He continues to represent peaceful, wide-eyed contemplation, seeing his images pass *before* him. The actor in his dramatized epic is still fundamentally a rhapsodist; the consecration of internal dreaming lies upon all his actions, so that he is never entirely an actor.[23]

What is the relationship between this ideal of Apolline drama and Euripidean tragedy? The same as that between the solemn rhapsodist of earlier times and the more recent kind, described as follows in Plato's *Ion*: 'If I say something sad, my eyes fill with tears; but if what I say is frightening and terrible, my hair stands on end with horror and my heart beats.' Now we can no longer see any trace of epic abandonment in illusion, the unemotional detachment of the true actor who, at the peak of the action, is entirely illusion and delight in illusion. Euripides is the actor with the beating heart, with his hair on end; he draws up the plan as a Socratic thinker, and puts it into effect as a passionate actor. He is a pure artist neither when drawing up the plan nor when putting it into effect. Thus the Euripidean tragedy is at once cool and fiery, capable both of freezing and of burning. It is incapable of achieving the Apolline effect of the epic, and has also made the greatest possible break with the Dionysiac elements, and now, in order to have any effect at all, it needs new stimuli which can no longer be found within either of these aesthetic impulses, neither the Apolline nor the Dionysiac. These stimuli are cool, paradoxical *thoughts* rather than Apolline contemplations, fiery *emotions* rather than Dionysiac ecstasies – and these thoughts and emotions are highly realistic counterfeits, by no means immersed in the ether of art.[24]

Now that we have recognized that Euripides failed absolutely in his efforts to base tragedy solely upon the Apolline spirit, and that his non-Dionysiac intention strayed into inartistic naturalism, we may approach the phenomenon of *aesthetic Socratism*, the chief law of which is, more or less: 'to be beautiful everything must first be intelligible' – a parallel to the Socratic dictum: 'only the one who knows is virtuous'. With this canon in his hand, Euripides weighed up each individual part – language, characters, dramatic construction, choral music – and adjusted it according to this criterion. What we are used to considering, in Euripides as against Sophocles, as a poetic shortcoming, a retrograde step, is generally the product of this insistent critical process, this audacious intelligibility. The Euripidean *prologue* may serve as an example of the productivity of this rationalistic method. Nothing could be more at odds with our stage technique than the prologue of the Euripidean drama. Having a character at the beginning of the play tell us who he is, what has preceded the action, what will happen in the course of the play – a modern stage-writer would describe this as a wilful and unforgivable repudiation of the effect of suspense. We know what is going to happen, so why should we wait until it actually does? After all, this is not the exciting relationship between a prophetic drama and a reality that will appear later on. Euripides thought quite differently. For him, the effect of tragedy never lay in epic tension, in the exciting uncertainty of what was going to happen now and afterwards: it lay rather in those great rhetorical-lyrical scenes in which the passion and dialectic of the protagonist swelled into a broad and mighty torrent. Everything prepared for pathos rather than plot. And everything that did not prepare for pathos was reprehensible. But the greatest obstacle of pleasurable participation in scenes such as these is a missing link for the listener, a gap in the mesh of the preceding story. As long as the listener is still obliged to work out what such and such a person means, what led up to such and such a conflict of inclinations and intentions, he cannot be completely immersed in the sufferings and actions of the protagonists, he cannot breathlessly participate in their suffering and fear. In their opening scenes Aeschylus and Sophocles employed the subtlest devices to give the spectator, as if by chance, all the threads that he would need for a complete understanding; a feature which preserves the noble artistry that masks the *necessary* formal element, making it look accidental. And yet Euripides thought he had observed that during those opening scenes the spectators grew peculiarly restless as they tried to work out what had gone before, so that they missed the poetic beauties and the pathos of the exposition. For that reason he placed the prologue before the exposition and put it in the mouth of someone who could be trusted: a deity often had to guarantee the course of the tragedy to the audience, and remove any doubt as to the reality of the myth – just as Descartes could only prove the reality of the empirical world by appealing to the veracity of God and His inability to lie. Euripides used this same divine veracity at the end of his drama, to guarantee the future of the protagonist to the audience. This was the purpose of the notorious *deus ex machina*. Between the epic preview and the epic prospect lies the dramatic-lyric present, the 'drama' itself.

As a poet, therefore, Euripides was first and foremost the echo of his conscious knowledge; and it is because of this that he has such a remarkable place in the history of Greek art. He must often have felt, with regard to his critical and productive work, that it was his duty to bring to dramatic life the beginning of Anaxagoras' treatise, which opens with the words: 'In the beginning everything was mixed together; then reason came and created order.' And if, with his *νοῦς*, Anaxagoras seemed to be the first sober philosopher in a company of drunkards, Euripides may well have seen himself in a similar relation to the other poets. While the sole regulator of all things, *νοῦς*, was excluded from artistic creation, everything was still mixed together in a chaotic primal soup. Euripides was obliged to hold his view, and as the first 'sober' poet he was obliged to condemn his 'drunken' peers. Sophocles' dictum about Aeschylus, that he did the right thing but unconsciously, was certainly not in accordance with Euripides' views: Euripides would have said that Aeschylus, *because* he worked unconsciously, worked wrongly. The divine Plato, too, generally speaks ironically of the poet's creative power, in so far as it is not a conscious insight, and places it on a par with the gift of the soothsayer and oneiromancer, since the poet is capable of writing only once he is unconscious and all reason has left him. Euripides, like Plato, set about showing the world the opposite of the 'irrational' poet; his aesthetic axiom, that 'everything must be conscious before it can be beautiful', is, as I have said, a counterpart to Socrates' axiom that 'everything must be conscious before it can be good'. Accordingly, Euripides became the poet of aesthetic Socratism. But Socrates was that *second spectator* who did not understand the older tragedy and therefore chose to ignore it; in league with him, Euripides dared to become the herald of a new creativity. If it was this that destroyed the older tragedy, then aesthetic Socratism is the principle behind its death. But in so far as the battle was directed against the Dionysiac elements of the older part, we may call Socrates the opponent of Dionysus, the new Orpheus who rose up against Dionysus and, although destined to be torn to pieces by the Maenads of the Athenian court, put the powerful god to flight. The god, as when he fled Lycurgus, king of the Edoni, escaped into the depths of the sea, the mystical floods of a secret cult that was gradually to cover the whole world.

13

That Socrates' aims were closely allied to those of Euripides did not escape their contemporaries in the ancient world. The most eloquent expression of this awareness is to be found in the story current in Athens, that Socrates used to help Euripides with his writing. Their names were mentioned in a single breath by the supporters of the 'good old days' whenever it came to enumerating the demagogues of the present. It was through their offices that the old robust Marathon soundness of body and mind was increasingly falling prey to a suspect enlightenment, involving a progressive atrophy of physical and mental forces. It was in this vein – half indignant, half contemptuous – that the comedies of

Aristophanes spoke of these men, to the horror of the new generation, which was quite willing to reject Euripides but could not get over the fact that Socrates appeared in the plays of Aristophanes as the chief of the *Sophists*, the epitome of everything that the Sophists were attempting to achieve. Their only consolation lay in pillorying Aristophanes himself as a dissolute and lying Alcibiades of poetry. Without wishing to defend the deep instincts of Aristophanes against such attacks, I shall proceed to demonstrate the close identity between Socrates and Euripides in the minds of the ancients; and it should not be forgotten that Socrates, an enemy of the art of tragedy, only ever attended performances of tragedies when a new play by Euripides was being performed. But the most famous example of the juxtaposition of the two names is to be found in the Delphic oracle which described Socrates as the wisest of men, but also awarded Euripides second prize in the contest of wisdom.

Sophocles was given third place in this ranking – Sophocles, who was able to claim, unlike Aeschylus, that he did the right thing because he *knew* what the right thing was. It is quite apparent that it was the lucidity of their *knowledge* that won these three men their reputation as the three 'ones who knew' of their day.

But the most acute statement about this radical new admiration for knowledge and insight came from Socrates, when he found that he alone admitted to himself that he *knew nothing*; while on his critical wanderings throughout Athens, addressing the greatest statesmen, rhetoricians, poets and artists, he encountered only the simulation of knowledge. He was astonished to realize that all those celebrities were lacking in a correct and secure insight even into their own professions, and carried out their work only instinctively. 'Only instinctively': the phrase touches the very heart and core of the Socratic intention. Socratism used it to depreciate all known art and ethics: wherever its piercing gaze alighted it found only a lack of insight and the power of delusion, and deduced from this that the prevailing situation was both misguided and reprehensible. Socrates believed that it was his mission to correct this state of affairs on the basis of this one point. He alone, with an air of irreverence and superiority, the precursor of a radically different culture, art and morality, entered a world whose coat-tails it would be our greatest privilege to touch.

That is what strikes us as so extraordinarily unsettling whenever we consider Socrates, and what constantly impels us to recognize the meaning and intention of that most dubious phenomenon of the classical age. Who would have the audacity single-handedly to deny the essence of Greece – which we know as Homer, Pindar and Aeschylus, as Phidias, Pericles, Pythia and Dionysus, as the deepest abyss and the highest summits – as worthy of our astonished veneration? What daemonic power could embolden anyone to throw this magic potion in the dust? What demigod, to whom the spirit chorus of the noblest of mankind must cry: 'Alas! With mighty fist you have destroyed the fair world; see, it falls, it crumbles!'[25]

One key to the nature of Socrates lies in that curious phenomenon known as Socrates' *daimonion*. In exceptional situations, when his tremendous intelligence faltered, he found guidance in a divine voice that spoke at such moments. That voice *admonishes* each time it comes. In this quite abnormal character, instinctive wisdom appears only to *hinder* conscious knowledge at certain points. While in all productive people instinct is the power of creativity and affirmation, and consciousness assumes a critical and dissuasive role, in Socrates instinct becomes the critic, consciousness the creator – a monstrosity *per defectum*! And what we see is a monster *defectus* of any mystical talent, so that Socrates might be described as the very embodiment of the *non-mystic*, whose logical nature has developed through superfetation, just as excessively as has instinctive wisdom in the mystic. On the other hand, however, no logical impulse in Socrates was able to turn against itself in the slightest; in this unbrooked torrent it showed a natural power such as we encounter only, to our awed astonishment, amongst the very greatest instinctive forces. Anyone who, in the writings of Plato, has experienced the merest hint of the divine *naïveté* and certainty of the Socratic life will also feel how the tremendous driving-wheel of logical Socratism is in motion *behind* Socrates, so to speak, and how it must be seen through Socrates as through a shadow. That he himself had an inkling of his state of affairs is apparent in the dignified gravity with which he defended his divine calling, even to his judges. It was no more possible to refute him than it was to approve of the corrosive influence he had on the instincts. In this irresolvable conflict, when he was brought before the forum of the Greek state, only one punishment was possible: exile. If they had sent this puzzling, uncategorizable, inexplicable phenomenon across the border, posterity could not have accused the Athenians of a disgraceful act. But Socrates himself seems to have insisted upon the pronouncement of a sentence of death rather than exile, with complete clarity of mind and without any natural awe of death. He went to his death as peacefully as, in Plato's description, he left the Symposium at daybreak, the last of the revellers, to begin a new day. While behind him, on the benches and the floor, his drowsy companions remained behind to dream of Socrates, the true eroticist. *The dying Socrates* became the new ideal for noble Greek youth: more than any other, the typical Hellenic youth, Plato, prostrated himself before the image with all the fervent devotion of his fanatic soul.[26]

14

Let us now imagine the great Cyclops eye of Socrates – that eye that had never glowed with the sweet madness of artistic inspiration – turned upon tragedy. Let us imagine that this eye had failed to gaze with pleasure into the abysses of the Dionysiac – what would it see in what Plato called the 'divine and praiseworthy' art of tragedy? Something utterly irrational, full of causes without apparent effects, effects without apparent cause; and all so diverse and many-hued that it would repel a sober temperament, but dangerously inflame sensitive and susceptible souls. As we know, the only poetic genre he understood was the *Aesopian fable*: and he did so with the same smiling acquiescence with which honest Gellert sings his praise of poetry in the fable of the bee and the hen:

Du siehst an mir, wozu sie nützt,
Dem, der nicht viel Verstand besitzt,
Die Wahrheit durch ein Bild zu sagen.

(You see in me what it can do,
In images, it tells what's true
To those without much wit.)

But for Socrates, tragedy did not even seem to 'tell what's true', quite apart from the fact that it addresses 'those without much wit', not the philosopher: another reason for giving it a wide berth. Like Plato, he numbered it among the flattering arts which represent only the agreeable, not the useful, and therefore required that his disciples abstain most rigidly from such unphilosophical stimuli – with such success that the young tragedian, Plato, burnt his writings in order to became a pupil of Socrates. But while indomitable innate talents might do battle with the Socratic maxims, they were always strong enough, as was their powerful author, to force poetry itself into new and unknown channels.

One example of this is Plato, whom we have just mentioned. In his condemnation of tragedy and art in general he did not lag behind his master's naïve cynicism, and yet from complete artistic necessity he had to create an art form that was related on a deep level to the art forms already in existence, which he repudiated. The main accusation that Plato levelled at the older art – that it was the counterfeit of an illusion and hence belonged to a sphere yet lower than the empirical world – must not apply to this new art: and thus we see Plato striving to go beyond reality and portray the idea at the basis of that pseudo-reality. But in the process Plato the thinker had taken a detour to arrive at a place where Plato the poet had always been at home – a place from which Sophocles and the whole of the older art solemnly protested against any accusations. If tragedy had absorbed all earlier genres within itself, the same might be said, in an eccentric sense, of the Platonic dialogue, which, a mixture of all available styles and forms, hovering somewhere between narrative, lyric poetry and drama, between prose and poetry, thus also infringed that strict older law of unified linguistic form. The *Cynic* writers went even further than this, until, with their brightly checkered style, their oscillation between prose and metric forms, they had attained the literary image of the 'raving Socrates' whom they represented in life. The Platonic dialogue might be described as the lifeboat in which the shipwrecked older poetry and all its children escaped: crammed together in a narrow space, fearfully obeying a single pilot, Socrates, they now entered a new world that could never tire of looking at this fantastic spectacle. Plato gave posterity the model for a new art form – the novel. This might be described as 'an infinitely enhanced Aesopian fable', in which poetry is subordinated to dialectical philosophy just as philosophy had for centuries been subordinated to theology – as an *ancilla*. This was the new channel into which Plato drove poetry, under the pressure of the daemonic Socrates.

Here *philosophical thought* overgrows art and forces it to cling tightly to the bough of the dialectic. The *Apolline* tendency is cocooned within its logical schematism; just as we found something similar in the work of Euripides, along with a translation of the Dionysiac into naturalistic emotions. Socrates, the dialectical hero of the Platonic drama, recalls the similar Euripidean hero, who is obliged to defend his actions with arguments and counter-arguments, and thus often runs the risk of forfeiting our tragic pity. For who could fail to recognize the optimistic element in the dialectic, which rejoices at each conclusion and can breathe only in cool clarity and consciousness: that optimistic element which, once it had invaded tragedy, gradually overgrew its Dionysiac regions and forced it into self-destruction – its death-leap into bourgeois theatre. We need only consider the Socratic maxims: 'Virtue is knowledge, all sins arise from ignorance, the virtuous man is the happy man.' In these three basic optimistic formulae lies the death of tragedy. For now the virtuous hero must be dialectical, there must be a necessary, visible bond between virtue and knowledge, faith and morality; the transcendental justice of Aeschylus is reduced to the flat and impudent principle of 'poetic justice', with its usual *deus ex machina*.

So how does the *chorus*, the whole musical and Dionysiac substratum of tragedy, look when compared to this new Socratic, optimistic stage-world? It looks arbitrary, an easily dispensable reminder of the origin of tragedy, although we have understood that the chorus can only be seen as the *cause* of tragedy and the tragic. This awkwardness is already apparent in Sophocles' treatment of the chorus – an indication that the Dionysiac basis of the tragedy was already beginning to crumble in his day. He no longer dares entrust the chorus with the bulk of the dramatic effect, but restricts its sphere to the point where it seems almost on a par with the actors, just as if it had been lifted from the orchestra on to the stage. In the process its essence is entirely destroyed, however much Aristotle might endorse this particular conception of the chorus. This disruption of the function of the chorus, which Sophocles recommended both in his dramatic practice and, tradition has it, even in an essay, is the first step towards the *annihilation* of the chorus, the phases of which were to succeed one another with frightening speed in Euripides, Agathon and the New Comedy. With the rod of its syllogisms the optimistic dialectic drives the music out of tragedy: it destroys the essence of tragedy, which can be interpreted only as a manifestation and illustration of Dionysiac states, as a visible symbolization of music, the dream world of a Dionysiac rapture.

Since we must, then, accept that even before Socrates there was an anti-Dionysiac tendency at work, and that Socrates was simply its most magnificent expression, we must not shirk the question of where such a phenomenon as Socrates was pointing. In the light of the Platonic dialogues, we cannot regard him merely as a negative agent of destruction. And just as the immediate effect of the Socratic impulse led inexorably to the dissolution of Dionysiac tragedy, a profound experience from the life of Socrates himself obliges us to ask whether there was necessarily a polar opposition between Socratism and art, and whether the idea of the birth of an 'artistic Socrates' is itself a contradiction in terms.

Where art was concerned, the despotic logician had the sense of a lacuna, a void, something of a reproach, of a possibly neglected duty. He told his friends in prison that he often had a dream in which he was told: 'Socrates, make music!' Until shortly before his death he drew comfort from the idea that his philosophy was the highest of the arts, spurning the notion that a deity might remind him of 'vulgar, popular music'. To salve his conscience entirely, he finally resolved in prison to make the very art he held in such low esteem. And with this attitude he wrote a hymn to Apollo and put some Aesopian fables into verse. It was something similar to the admonishing voice of his daemon that urged him to carry out these exercises, his Apolline realization that, like a barbarian king, he was unable to understand a noble divine image, and risked blaspheming that deity by his incomprehension. This voice of the Socratic dream vision is the only indication that he ever gave any consideration to the limitations of logic. He was obliged to ask: 'Is that which is unintelligible to me necessarily unintelligent? Might there be a realm of wisdom from which the logician is excluded? Might art even be a necessary correlative and supplement to science?'

15

In the light of these suggestive questions we must now explain how the influence of Socrates, up to our own times and beyond, has spread across posterity like a shadow lengthening in the evening sun, and how it has continually led to the regeneration of art – in the broadest and deepest, metaphysical sense – and by its own infinity guarantees the infinity of art.

Before we were able to recognize this, before we could convincingly demonstrate the most intimate dependence of all art on the Greeks, from Homer to Socrates, we had to do to the Greeks what the Athenians did to Socrates. Practically all eras and stages of civilization have tried, with profound displeasure, to free themselves from the Greeks, because all their own achievements, everything supposedly original and thoroughly admired suddenly seemed to lose colour and life in comparison, shrivelling into a poor copy, a caricature. And once again there would be an outburst of cordial fury with that presumptuous little nation that dared to brand everything that was not native to it as 'barbaric' for all time. Who were those people, they asked, who, although their historic splendour was ephemeral, their institutions ridiculously restricted and their moral competence questionable, although, indeed, they practised disagreeable vices, could still lay claim to dignity and pre-eminence among nations as genius does amongst the masses? Sadly, the cup of hemlock with which such a creature might be dispatched was not forthcoming. For the poison compounded from envy, slander and rage was not enough to destroy that self-sufficient glory. And so we feel both shame and fear before the Greeks; although some, valuing truth above all else, have dared confess the truth: that the Greeks are the charioteers of our own and all other cultures, but that the chariot and the horses are almost always of too poor a quality, not a match for the glory of the drivers, who then make sport of driving the team into the abyss – clearing it themselves with a leap of Achilles.

If we wish to consider Socrates as one of these charioteers, we need only see him as the prototype of a new and unimagined life-form, the prototype of *theoretical man*. Our next task must be to understand the significance and purpose of that figure. Like the artist, theoretical man takes an infinite delight in everything that exists, and, like him, he is shielded by that delight from the practical ethics of pessimism with its eyes of Lynceus that glow only in the dark. Whenever the truth is uncovered, the artist gazes enraptured at whatever covering remains, but theoretical man takes delight and satisfaction in the covering that has been cast aside, and takes his greatest delight in a process of uncovering that is always successful and always achieved by his own efforts. Science would not exist if it were concerned only with that *one* naked goddess. For then its adepts would feel like people trying to dig a hole through the centre of the earth: each of them realizing that, toil though he might his whole life long, he could dig through only the smallest fraction of that immense depth, and that even that would be covered over by his neighbour's efforts, so that a third man would be well advised to find a new spot for his tunnelling. If another were now to prove that the antipodes could not be reached by such a direct route, would anyone go on digging in the old spot unless for the incidental pleasure of finding precious stones or discovering natural laws? For this reason

Lessing, the most honest of theoretical men, dared to say that he took greater delight in the quest for truth than in the truth itself. He thus revealed the fundamental secret of science, to the astonishment and irritation of scientists. Alongside this isolated acknowledgement, an excess of honesty or even high spirits, there is a profound *illusion* which first entered the world in the person of Socrates – the unshakeable belief that rational thought, guided by causality, can penetrate to the depths of being, and that it is capable not only of knowing but even of *correcting* being. This sublime metaphysical illusion is an instinctual accompaniment to science, and repeatedly takes it to its limits, where it must become *art*: *which is the true purpose of this mechanism*.

Bearing the torch of this thought, let us now consider Socrates. We will see him as the first man who was able not only to live by this instinct of science but – a far greater accomplishment – to die by it as well. That is why the image of the *dying Socrates*, man freed by insight and reason from the fear of death, became the emblem over the portals of science, reminding all who entered of their mission: to make existence appear intelligible and consequently justified. And if reason proves insufficient, the *myth* must also be invoked – the myth which I described above as the necessary consequence, indeed the purpose, of science.

Let us consider how after Socrates, the mystagogue of science, waves of philosophical schools emerged and vanished one after the other; how a thirst for knowledge hitherto unimagined throughout the educated world, the true task for everyone of superior intelligence, led science on to the high seas from which it has never been entirely banished; how that universality first established a common network of rational thought across the globe, providing glimpses of the lawfulness of an entire solar system. Once we remember this, and the astonishingly high pyramid of knowledge of the present day, we cannot help but see Socrates as the turning-point, the vortex of world history. For if we imagine that the whole incalculable store of energy used in that global tendency had been used *not* in the service of knowledge but in ways applied to the practical – selfish – goals of individuals and nations, universal wars of destruction and constant migrations of peoples would have enfeebled man's instinctive zest for life to the point where, suicide having become universal, the individual would perhaps feel a vestigial duty as a son to strangle his parents, or as a friend his friend, as the Fiji islanders do: a practical pessimism that could even produce a terrible ethic of genocide through pity, and which is, and always has been, present everywhere in the world where art has not in some form, particularly as religion and science, appeared as a remedy and means of prevention for this breath of pestilence.

In the face of this practical pessimism, Socrates is the archetype of the theoretical optimist who, in his faith in the explicability of the nature of things, attributes the power of a panacea to knowledge and science, and sees error as the embodiment of evil. To penetrate those arguments and separate true knowledge from illusion and error seemed to Socratic man the noblest, or even the only, truly human calling: just as the mechanism of concepts, judgements and conclusions, from Socrates onwards, was deemed the supreme activity, the most admirable gift of nature above all other talents. Even the most sublime noble deeds, the emotions of pity, sacrifice, heroism and that spiritual calm, so hard to attain, which the Apolline Greeks called *Sophrosyne*, were seen by Socrates and his like-minded successors, through to the present day, as being derived from the dialectic of knowledge, and hence were described as teachable. No one who has experienced the delight of Socratic knowledge, and sensed how, in ever-wider circles, it seeks to encompass the whole phenomenal world, will ever again find a stimulus to existence more compelling than the desire to complete that conquest, and weave the net to an impenetrable density. To anyone who thinks in such terms, the Platonic Socrates appears as the teacher of a quite new form of 'Greek cheerfulness' and blissful delight in life, which seeks to discharge itself in actions – most often in maieutic and pedagogical influences on noble youths, with the aim of finally producing genius.

But now, spurred on by its powerful illusion, science is rushing irresistibly to its limits, where the optimism essential to logic collapses. For the periphery of the circle of science has an infinite number of points, and while it is as yet impossible to tell how the circle could ever be fully measured, the noble, gifted man, even before the mid-course of his life, inevitably reaches that peripheral boundary, where he finds himself staring into the ineffable. If he sees here, to his dismay, how logic twists around itself and finally bites itself in the tail, there dawns a new form of knowledge, tragic knowledge, which needs art as both protection and remedy, if we are to bear it.

Let us turn our eyes, which now are refreshed and fortified by the Greeks, to the highest spheres of the world that flows around us. We shall see the insatiable, optimistic zest for knowledge, exemplified in the figure of Socrates, transformed into tragic resignation and a need for art; while that same zest, at its lower levels, must express itself in terms hostile to art, and find Dionysiac tragedy profoundly repellent, as we have seen in the battle between Aeschylean tragedy and Socratism.

We now knock agitatedly at the portals of the present and the future; will that 'transformation' lead to ever-new configurations of genius, and particularly of the *music-making Socrates*? Will the net of art that is spread over existence, whether in the name of religion or science, be woven ever more solidly and delicately, or is it doomed to be torn to shreds beneath the restless, barbaric hubbub that is 'the present'? Let us stand aside for a while, concerned but not inconsolable, like contemplative men who are allowed to be witnesses of those tremendous battles and transitions. Alas – such is the magic of those battles that all who witness them must also join the fray![27]

16

We have tried with this historical example to explain how tragedy perishes when deprived of the spirit of music just as sure as it can be born only of that spirit. To mitigate the strangeness of this claim, and to demonstrate the origin of this insight, we must now frankly consider similar phenomena in the present. We must stride boldly into the thick of those battles which, as I have said, are being waged in the highest spheres of the contemporary world between insatiable optimistic knowledge and the tragic need for art. I shall ignore all the other hostile impulses which, in any age, work against art in general and tragedy in particular, and which in our own time, too, are gaining ground with every confidence of victory – so much so that among the theatrical arts, for example, only the farce and the ballet have flourished with any luxuriance, sprouting blossoms that might not smell sweet to everyone. I wish to speak only of the most *illustrious antagonist* of the tragic view of the world, science, which is optimistic to the very core, with its ancestor Socrates at its head. And I shall then name the forces that seem to me to harbour within them a *rebirth of tragedy* – and who knows what other blissful hopes for the German spirit!

Before we rush into the fray, let us gird ourselves with the knowledge that we have won so far. Unlike all those who seek to infer the arts from a single principle, the necessary spring of life for every work of art, I shall fix my gaze on those two artistic deities of the Greeks, Apollo and Dionysus. For me they are the vivid and concrete representations of *two* worlds of art, utterly different in their deepest essence and their highest aims. Apollo I see as the transfiguring genius of the *principium individuationis*, the sole path to true redemption through illusion. While in the mystical triumphal cry of Dionysus the spell of individuation is broken and the path is opened to the Mothers of Being, to the innermost core of things. This tremendous opposition, this yawning abyss between the Apolline plastic arts and Dionysiac music, became so obvious to one of our great thinkers that even without the guidance of the divine Hellenic symbols he said that music differed in character and origin from all the other arts, because unlike them it was not a replica of phenomena, but the direct replica of the will itself, and complemented *everything physical in the world* with a representation of the thing-in-itself, *the metaphysical* (Schopenhauer, *World as Will and Representation*, I [p. 262]). Richard Wagner has fixed his seal on this most important insight in the whole of aesthetics (which signals, in a serious sense, the beginning of aesthetics), establishing in this essay *Beethoven* that music obeys quite different aesthetic principles from the visual arts, and cannot be measured according to the category of beauty; although a false aesthetic, hand in hand with a misdirected and degenerate art, has grown used to demanding, on the basis of the concept of beauty that prevails in the world of the visual arts, that music should provide an effect similar to that of works in the visual arts – the arousal of *pleasure in beautiful forms*. Once I had become aware of this tremendous contrast I felt strongly compelled to approach the essence of Greek tragedy and thus the most profound manifestation of the Hellenic genius. For only now did I feel myself in possession of a charm which would enable me to go beyond the phraseology of conventional aesthetics and clearly represent to myself the essential problem of tragedy. This afforded me such a unique and surprising glimpse into the Greek spirit that I felt that our classical philology, for all its proud gestures, had hitherto sustained itself only on shadow-plays and externals.

We might touch upon that essential problem by asking this question: what is the aesthetic effect that arises when the divided aesthetic powers of the Apolline and the Dionysiac are made to work side by side? Or to put it more concisely: how is music related to image and concept? Schopenhauer, praised by Richard Wagner for expressing that very point with unsurpassed clarity, presents the issue most clearly in the following passage, which I shall reproduce in full:

As a result of all this, we can consider the phenomenal world, or nature, and music as two different expressions of the same thing, which is therefore the only medium of the analogy that connects them, a knowledge of which is required if we are to understand that analogy. Accordingly, music, if it is regarded as an expression of the world, is in the highest degree a universal language that is even related to the universality of concepts much as those concepts are related to particular things. Yet its universality is by no means the empty universality of abstraction, but is of a quite different kind, connected with thorough and clear distinctness. In this respect it is like geometrical figures and numbers, which are the universal forms of all possible objects of experience, *a priori* applicable to them all, and yet are not abstract, but perceptible and thoroughly definite. All possible efforts, stirrings, and expressions of the will, all the events that occur within man himself and are included by the faculty of reason in the wide, negative concept of feeling, can be expressed by the infinite number of possible melodies, but always in the universality of mere form without the material, always only according to the in-itself, not according to the phenomenon, as we might say the innermost soul of the phenomenon without the body. This close relation between music and the true nature of all things can also explain the fact that, when music suitable to any scene, action, event or environment is played, it seems to disclose to us its most secret meaning, and appears to be the most accurate and distinct commentary upon it. Moreover, to anyone who abandons himself entirely to the impression of a symphony, it is as if he can see all the possible events of life and of the world passing by within himself. Yet if he reflects, he cannot assert any likeness between that piece of music and the things that passed through his mind. For, as we have said, music differs from all the other arts in that it is not a copy of the phenomenon, or, more exactly, of the will's adequate objectivity, but is directly a copy of the will itself, and therefore expresses the metaphysical to everything physical in the world, the thing-in-itself to every phenomenon. Accordingly, we might just as well call the world embodied music as embodied will; for this reason music makes every painting, indeed every scene from real life and from the world, at once appear in enhanced significance, and this is, of course, all the greater, the more analogous its melody is to the inner spirit of the given phenomenon. It is because of this that we are able to set a poem to music as a song, or a perceptive representation as a pantomime, or both as an opera. Such individual pictures of human life, set to the universal language of music, are never bound to it, never correspond to it with absolute necessity, but relate to it only as an example relates to a universal concept. In the distinctness of reality they represent what music asserts in the universality of mere form. For, to a certain extent, melodies are, like universal concepts, an abstraction from reality. This reality, and hence the world of individual things, furnishes what is perceptive, special and individual, the particular case, both to the universality of the concepts and to that of melodies. These two universalities, however, are in a certain respect opposed to each other, since the concepts contain only the forms, first of all abstracted from perception, we might say the stripped-off outer shell of things; hence they are quite properly *abstracta*. Music, on the other hand, provides the innermost kernel preceding all form, or the heart of things. This relation could very well be expressed in the language of the scholastics by saying that the concepts are the *universalia post rem*, but music gives the *universalia ante rem*, and reality the *universalia in re*. But that in general a relation between a composition and a perceptive representation is possible is due, as we have said, to the fact that the two are simply quite different expressions of the same inner nature of the world. If now, in the particular case, such a relation actually exists, thus when the composer has known how to express in the universal language of music the stirrings of will that constitute the kernel of an event, then the melody of the song, the music of the opera, is expressive. But the analogy discovered by the composer between these two must have come from the immediate knowledge of the inner nature of the world unknown to his faculty of reason; it cannot be an imitation brought about with conscious intention by means of concepts, otherwise the music does not express the inner essence, the will itself, but merely provides an inadequate imitation of its phenomenon inadequately. All really imitative music does this.

(*World as Will and Representation*, I [p. 262])

According to Schopenhauer's theory, then, we see music as the immediate language of the will, and feel our imagination impelled to give form to the spirit world that speaks to us, invisible and yet vitally stirring, and embody it in an analogous example. On the other hand, image and concept, influenced by a truly corresponding music, attain a higher level of significance. Thus Dionysiac art tends to exert two kinds of influence on the Apolline artistic faculty: music encourages a *symbolic intuition* of Dionysiac universality, and then endows that symbolic image with *the highest level of significance*. From these facts, quite intelligible in themselves and not inaccessible to deeper consideration, we can conclude that music can give birth to *the myth*, that most significant of examples, and the *tragic* myth above all: the myth that speaks symbolically of the Dionysiac wisdom. I have shown, in the phenomenon of the lyric poet, how music strives to make its essence known in Apolline images: bearing in mind that music, at its highest level, must also seek to attain its highest expression in images, we must consider it possible that it can also find the symbolic expression of its actual Dionysiac wisdom. And where else should we seek this expression if not in tragedy, and in the concept of the *tragic*?

The tragic cannot be honestly inferred from the nature of art as it is conventionally conceived, according to the single category of illusion and beauty. Only from the spirit of music can we understand delight in the destruction of the individual. For only in single instances of such destruction can we clearly see the eternal phenomenon of Dionysiac art, which expresses the will in its omnipotence, behind the *principium individuationis*, the eternal life that lies beyond the phenomenal world, regardless of all destruction. Metaphysical delight in the tragic is a translation of the image: the hero, the supreme manifestation of the will, is negated to our gratification, because he is only a phenomenon, and the eternal life of the will is left untouched by his destruction. 'We believe in eternal life' is tragedy's cry; while music is the immediate idea of that life. The purpose of the plastic arts is quite different: here Apollo overcomes the suffering of the individual by means of the luminescent glorification of the *eternity of the phenomenon*; beauty triumphs over the suffering inherent in life; pain is, in a certain sense, deluded away from amongst the features of nature.[28] In Dionysiac art and its tragic symbolism, the same nature addresses us with its true, undisguised voice: 'Be like me! The Primal Mother, eternally creative, eternally impelling into life, eternally drawing satisfaction from the ceaseless flux of phenomena!'

17

Dionysiac art, too, wishes to convince us of the eternal delight of existence – but we are to seek that delight not in phenomena themselves but behind phenomena. It wishes us to acknowledge that everything that comes into being must be prepared to face a sorrowful end. It forces us to look at the terrors of individual existence, yet we are not to be petrified with fear. A metaphysical consolation wrests us momentarily from the bustle of changing forms. For a brief moment we really become the primal essence itself, and feel its unbounded lust for existence and delight in existence. Now we see the struggles, the torment, the destruction of phenomena as necessary, given the constant proliferation of forms of existence forcing and pushing their way into life, the exuberant fertility of the world will. We are pierced by the raging goad of those torments just as we become one with the vast primal delight in existence and sense the eternity of that delight in

Dionysiac ecstasy. For all our pity and terror, we are happy to be alive, not as individuals but as *the* single living thing, merged with its creative delight.

The story of the origin of Greek tragedy now tells us with brilliant precision how the tragic art of the Greeks was really born out of the spirit of music, and our understanding helps us for the first time to do justice to the primitive and astounding significance of the chorus. But we must admit that the meaning of the tragic myth was never transparent in all its conceptual clarity to the Greek poets, let alone to the Greek philosophers. To a certain extent, their heroes speak more superficially than they act. Myth does not find adequate objectification in the spoken word. The structure of the scenes and the visible images reveal a deeper wisdom than the poet himself can convey in words and concepts. We find the same thing in Shakespeare, whose Hamlet, for example, likewise speaks more superficially than he acts, so that the lesson of *Hamlet*, which we have already mentioned, is to be found not in the words themselves but in a profound contemplation and survey of the play as a whole. As regards Greek tragedy, which we of course encounter only as a verbal drama, I have even suggested that the incongruity between myth and word can easily mislead us into thinking it shallower and less significant than it really is, and to expect from it a more superficial effect than it must have had, to judge by the testimonies of the ancients. For it is so easily forgotten that where the poet failed in his attempts to achieve the supreme spiritualization and ideal of the myth, he was constantly successful as a musician! Of course we must reconstruct the overwhelming power of the musical effect in an almost scholarly fashion before we perceive anything of the incomparable consolation that must have been inherent in true tragedy. But only if we were Greeks would we properly appreciate even that musical power, while in the whole of Greek music – compared with the infinitely richer music with which we are so familiar – we can hear only the youthful song of the genius of music, its sense of power modestly intoned. The Greeks are, as the Egyptian priests say, eternal children, and even in tragic art they are only children, ignorant of the sublime plaything which has come into being in their hands, and which will soon be shattered.

The striving of the spirit of music for visual and mythical revelation, growing in intensity from the beginnings of lyric poetry to Attic tragedy, suddenly breaks off after its first luxuriant development, and disappears, we might say, from the surface of Hellenic art; while the Dionysiac philosophy born of that same striving lives on in the mysteries, and even in its most alarming metamorphoses and distortions never ceases to attract more serious minds. Will it not rise again from its mystical depths, as art?

Here we are concerned with the question of whether the opposing power to which tragedy succumbed will always have the strength to obstruct the artistic reawakening of tragedy and the tragic philosophy. If the tragedy of the ancients was diverted from its course by the dialectical impulse towards knowledge and scientific optimism, we might conclude from this that there is a never-ending struggle between the theoretical and the tragic philosophies. And only after the scientific spirit has been taken to its limits, and has been forced by the demonstration of those limits to renounce its claim to universal validity, can we hope for a rebirth of tragedy. We might employ the symbol of the *music-making Socrates*, in the sense discussed earlier, to describe that cultural form. In this contrast, I see the spirit of science as that faith in the explicability of nature and the universal healing powers of knowledge which first came to light in the person of Socrates.

Bearing in mind the immediate consequences of this restlessly inquiring scientific spirit, we immediately recall how it destroyed the *myth*, and how that destruction uprooted poetry from its natural, ideal soil, leaving it homeless. If we are right to grant music the power of giving birth to the myth once more, we shall also be obliged to seek the spirit of science in those places where it attacked the mythopoeic power of music. One such occurs in the development of the *New Attic Dithyramb*, whose music no longer expressed the inner essence, the will itself, but only unsatisfactorily reproduced phenomena in a conceptual and imitative form. Truly musical natures spurned that profoundly degenerate music with just the same distaste that they felt for the anti-artistic tendencies of Socrates. The unerring and incisive instinct of Aristophanes had certainly grasped the key when he lumped together Socrates himself, Euripidean tragedy and the music of the New Dithyrambic poets with the same feeling of hatred, and sensed the symptoms of a degenerate culture in all three phenomena. The New Dithyramb sacrilegiously degraded music into an imitative counterfeit of phenomena – of battle, for example, or a storm at sea – and thus robbed it of all its mythopoeic power. For if it seeks to delight us solely by compelling us to seek superficial analogies between a process in life and nature and certain rhythmical figures and musical sounds, if our intellect is supposed to be satisfied by the recognition of those analogies, we can no longer be in a condition to respond to the mythical. For the myth wishes to be seen as a unique example of a universality and truth that gazes into infinity. Truly Dionysiac music is just such a general mirror of the universal will. Every concrete event reflected in this mirror is immediately broadened out for our emotions into the illustration of an eternal truth. Conversely, any such concrete event is immediately stripped of all mythical character by the tone-painting of the New Dithyramb. Now that music has become the paltry replica of a phenomenon, it is infinitely poorer than the phenomenon itself. This poverty is such that it reduces the phenomenon in our consciousness, so that now, for example, a battle imitated by music is exhausted in march rhythms, battle cries and so on, and our imagination is permitted to go no further than these superficial features. Thus tone-painting is in every respect the opposite of the mythopoeic power of true music. It renders phenomena poorer than they are, while Dionysiac music extends and enriches the individual phenomenon into an image of the universe. The non-Dionysiac spirit enjoyed a mighty victory when, in the development of the New Dithyramb, it estranged music from itself and made it a slave to the phenomenon. Euripides, whom we might call an utterly unmusical nature, although in a higher sense, was for this very reason a passionate devotee of the New Dithyrambic music, and deploys all its effects and manners with a robber's generosity.

Looking in another direction, we can see the power of this anti-mythic, non-Dionysiac spirit in action if we turn our attention to the increased stress on *character portrayal* and psychological refinement that occurs in Sophoclean tragedy. The character is no longer expected to broaden out into an eternal archetype, but rather to come across as an individual, with artificial characteristics and nuances, each trait most precisely determined, so that the spectator is no longer alive to the myth and instead focuses on the verisimilitude of the characterization and the artist's mimetic power. Here, too, we are aware of the victory of the individual phenomenon over the universal, and the delight taken in the study of an individual anatomical specimen, as it were; we are already breathing the air of a theoretical world in which scientific knowledge is esteemed more highly than the artistic reflection of a universal law. This tendency towards characterization proceeds apace: while Sophocles still paints whole characters, and subjugates the myth for their refined development, Euripides paints only broad individual traits of character, expressed in violent passions. In the New Attic Comedy all that remains is masks with a *single* expression -- frivolous old men, duped panders, mischievous slaves -- tirelessly repeated. What has become of the mythopoeic spirit of music? The only music that remains is designed either to excite or to provoke reminiscence, either a stimulant for dulled, exhausted nerves, or tone-painting. The former is barely concerned with the accompanying text: even the songs of Euripidean heroes and choruses are fairly slovenly; how bad can it get in the work of his impudent successors?

But the new non-Dionysiac spirit is most clearly apparent in the *endings* of the new dramas. At the end of the old tragedies there was a sense of metaphysical conciliation without which it is impossible to imagine our taking delight in tragedy; perhaps the conciliatory tones from another world echo most purely in *Oedipus at Colonus*. Now, once tragedy had lost the genius of music, tragedy in the strictest sense was dead: for where was that metaphysical consolation now to be found? Hence an earthly resolution for tragic dissonance was sought; the hero, having been adequately tormented by fate, won his well-earned reward in a stately marriage and tokens of divine honour. The hero had become a gladiator, granted freedom once he had been satisfactorily flayed and scarred. Metaphysical consolation had been ousted by the *deus ex machina*.

I do not mean that tragic philosophy was thoroughly and universally destroyed by the encroaching non-Dionysiac spirit: but we do know that it had to flee the sphere of art for the underworld, as it were, in the degenerate form of a secret cult. Meanwhile the consuming breath of that spirit raged over the whole surface of the Hellenic world, manifested in the form of 'Greek cheerfulness' which we earlier described as an aged and unproductive delight in existence. This cheerfulness is opposed to the glorious *naïveté* of the earlier Greeks, the flower of Apolline culture that arose from the gloomy abyss, the triumph of the Greek will, won by its reflection of beauty, over suffering and the wisdom of suffering. The noblest form of the other form of 'Greek cheerfulness', the Alexandrian, is the cheerfulness of *theoretical man*: it manifests the same features that I have inferred from the spirit of the non-Dionysiac – it opposes Dionysiac wisdom and art, it seeks to destroy the myth, replaces metaphysical consolation with an earthly consonance, a *deus ex machina* of its own – the god of machines and crucibles, the powers of the spirits of nature acknowledged and employed in the services of the higher egoism; it believes in the rectification of the world through knowledge and in a life guided by science, and it can also truly confine the individual within a limited circle of soluble problems, from which he can cheerfully say to life: 'I want you. You are worth knowing.'

18

It is an eternal phenomenon: the voracious will always finds a way to keep its creations alive and perpetuate their existence, by casting an illusion over things. One man will be enthralled by Socratic delight in knowledge and the delusion that it might heal the eternal wound of existence, while another will be caught up in the seductive veil of beauty, art, that floats before his eyes, and yet another will be gripped by the metaphysical consolation that beneath the whirlpool of phenomena eternal life flows indestructibly onwards: not to mention the more common and perhaps yet more powerful illusions that the will keeps constantly in readiness.

These three levels of illusion are meant only for those nobler spirits who experience the burden and weight of existence more profoundly, and who must be deluded away from their distress with special stimulants. That which we call culture is made up entirely of those stimulants. According to the proportions of the mixture, culture is predominantly Socratic or artistic or tragic; or if we may be permitted historical exemplifications, Alexandrian, Hellenic or Indian (Brahman).

The whole of our modern world is caught up in the net of Alexandrian culture, and its ideal is theoretical man, armed with the highest powers of knowledge and working in the service of science, whose archetype and progenitor is Socrates. All of our educational methods take their bearings from this ideal: any other form of existence has a hard struggle to survive alongside it, and is in the end tolerated rather than encouraged. In an almost frightening sense, the man of culture has long existed only in the form of the scholar; even our poetic arts have had to develop from scholarly imitations, and in the principal effect of rhyme we can still recognize the origin of our own poetic in artificial experiments with a non-native, indeed a scholarly language. How unintelligible to a true Greek must *Faust* appear, the modern man of culture, intelligible in himself, as he storms unsatisfied through all the faculties, devoting himself to magic and the devil because of his urge for knowledge. We need only compare him with Socrates to see that modern man has begun to sense the limitations of the Socratic delight in knowledge, and yearns for a shore from the wide and barren sea of knowledge. When Goethe said to Eckermann, on the subject of Napoleon: 'Yes, my friend, there is also a productivity of deeds', he was reminding us, in a charmingly naïve way, that non-theoretical man is incredible and astonishing to modern man. We need the wisdom of a Goethe before we can find such an alien form of life comprehensible, or indeed forgivable.

And we should be fully aware of what lies at the heart of that Socratic culture – optimism, imagining itself boundless! We should not be afraid when the fruits of that optimism ripen; when society, leavened from top to bottom by such a culture, slowly begins to quake with extravagant surges and yearnings; when belief in the earthly happiness of all men, belief in the possibility of such a universal culture of knowledge, is slowly transformed into the menacing demand for such an Alexandrian earthly happiness, the evocation of a Euripidean *deus ex machina*! It should be noted: Alexandrian culture needs a slave class in order to exist in the long term; but in its optimistic view of existence it denies the necessity of such a class and therefore, once the effect of its fine seductive and consoling words about 'the dignity of man' and 'the dignity of labour' has worn off, it slowly drifts towards terrible destruction. There is nothing more terrible than a barbaric slave class that has learned to consider its existence an injustice and sets about taking its revenge, not only on its own behalf, but on behalf of all past generations. Who, faced with such lowering storms, would dare appeal to our pallid and weary religions, which have degenerated in their fundamentals into scholarly religions? Myth, the prerequisite for all religions, is already thoroughly paralysed, and even theology is dominated by that very optimistic spirit that we have just described as the germ of destruction of our society.

While the blight that lies dormant in the womb of theoretical culture is gradually beginning to frighten modern man, and he casts uneasily around in the stores of his experience for remedies to ward off the danger without quite believing in their efficacy, while he begins to have an inkling of the consequences of his situation, great and universally minded spirits have, with incredible level-headedness, used the armoury of science to lay bare the limitations and determinations of knowledge, and have thus decisively negated the claims of science to universal validity and universal goals. In so doing, they have revealed the delusion, based on the principle of causality, which imagines it can explain the innermost essence of things. The tremendous courage and wisdom of *Kant* and *Schopenhauer* carried off the most difficult victory: victory over the optimism that lurked within the essence of logic, which in turn forms the basis of our culture. Where that optimism had believed that all the mysteries of the world could be known and explained, relying on apparently innocuous *aeternae veritates*, and had treated space, time and causality as utterly unconditional and universally valid laws, Kant revealed how these in fact only served to transform mere phenomena, the work of Maya, into the sole true essence of things, and thus render true knowledge of that essence thoroughly impossible. Or, as Schopenhauer has it, to send the dreamer into an even deeper sleep (*World as Will and Representation*, I). This insight ushered in a culture which I should like to call tragic. Its most important characteristic is that its highest goal lies no longer in science but in wisdom, undeceived by the enticing diversions of the sciences; that it turns a steady eye on the world as a whole, and seeks to grasp, with a sympathetic love, eternal suffering as its own.

Let us imagine a rising generation with such an undaunted gaze, with such a heroic proclivity for the tremendous. Let us imagine the bold stride of those dragon-slayers, the proud audacity with which they turn their backs on all the weaklings' doctrines that lie within that optimism, in order to 'live resolutely' in all that they do. *Must* the tragic man in that culture, trained through his self-education for seriousness and terror, not inevitably yearn for a new *art of metaphysical consolation*, tragedy, as his Helen, and to exclaim as Faust did:

> Und sollt' ich nicht, sehnsüchtigster Gewalt,
> Ins Leben ziehn die einzigste Gestalt?[29]
>
> (And should I not with utmost yearning seek
> To bring to life that creature most unique?)

But now that Socratic culture has been shaken from two directions; now that it can only hold the sceptre of its infallibility with trembling hands – both out of fear of its own consequences, which it is just beginning to foresee, and also because it has lost its former confidence in the eternal validity of its foundations – it is sad to see the dance of its thought rush longingly to embrace new forms one after the other, only to let them go in horror, as Mephistopheles did the seductive Lamiae. That is the characteristic of the 'breach' commonly said to be the fundamental ailment of modern culture: theoretical man takes fright at his consequences, and in his dissatisfaction no longer dares to hurl himself into the terrible icy current of existence, but runs nervously up and down on the bank. He no longer wants anything whole, with all the natural cruelty that adheres to things, so coddled has he been by optimism. At the same time, he feels how a culture based on the principle of science must perish once it begins to become *illogical*, to flee its own consequences. This universal misery is apparent in our art. In vain do we imitatively depend on all the great productive periods and spirits; in vain does the whole of 'world literature' gather around modern man as a consolation to him; in vain is he set in the midst of artistic styles and artists of all the ages so that he may name them as Adam named the animals. He remains eternally hungry, the 'critic' without pleasure or strength, Alexandrian man, at bottom a librarian and a corrector of proofs, wretchedly blinded by the dust of his tomes and by printing errors.

19

We cannot describe the innermost content of this Socratic culture more accurately than by calling it *the culture of opera*. For it is in this area that this culture has voiced its desires and perceptions with a *naïveté* all its own, which is surprising if we compare the genesis of opera and the history of its development with the eternal truths of the Apolline and the Dionysiac. I should like first of all to remind the reader of the origin of the *stilo rappresentativo* and the recitative. Is it conceivable that the music of opera, thoroughly externalized and incapable of reverence, should have been enthusiastically welcomed and cherished, as the rebirth, so to speak, of all true magic, by an age that had just produced the ineffably sublime and sacred music of Palestrina? And who, on the other hand, would attribute the wild spread of the love of opera solely to the luxuriousness of the diversion-seeking Florentine circles and the vanity of their dramatic singers? I can only explain the fact that this passion for a half-musical 'speech' arose in the same age, indeed among the same people, alongside the vaulted arches of Palestrina's harmonies, which the whole of the Christian Middle Ages had helped to build, with reference to an *extra-artistic tendency* which contributed to the essence of the recitative.

The singer accommodates the listener who wishes to hear the words distinctly beneath the music, by speaking more than singing, and by intensifying the dramatic expression of the words with this half-song. By thus intensifying the pathos he makes the words easier to understand, and overcomes the other half of the music. He now runs the risk of the music becoming predominant at an inopportune moment, immediately destroying the pathos of the speech and the distinctness of the words, while he feels a constant impulse towards musical discharge and a virtuoso presentation of his vocal abilities. Here the 'poet' comes to his aid, providing him with ample opportunities for lyrical interjections, repetitions of words, sentences and so on, at which points the singer, now in the purely musical element, can relax without consideration for the words. This alternation of emotionally charged speech, only partly sung, and wholly sung interjections, the basis of *stilo rappresentativo*, this rapidly alternating attempt to affect now the listener's attentiveness to concept and idea, and now his musical response, is both so utterly unnatural and so profoundly contradictory of the Apolline and Dionysiac artistic impulses that we must infer an origin of the recitative in something extrinsic to all artistic instincts. According to this description, the recitative might be defined as a mixture of epic and lyrical declamation; not a profoundly stable mixture, which could not be achieved from such thoroughly diverse components, but a highly external, mosaic-like conglutination entirely without parallel in the world of nature and experience. *But this was not the opinion of the inventors of recitative*: they themselves, and along with them their own times, believed that *stilo rappresentativo* had solved the mystery of ancient music, the secret that alone was able to explain the enormous effect of Orpheus, Amphion and even of Greek tragedy. The new style was held to be the reawakening of the most effective music, the music of ancient Greece; indeed, given the general and quite traditional view of the Homeric world *as the primal world*, they were able to succumb to the dream that they had returned to mankind's beginnings in paradise, when music too must necessarily have had that unparalleled purity, power and innocence of which the poets spoke so movingly in their pastoral plays. This allows us to see to the heart of the development of that truly modern genre, opera: here art is responding to a powerful need, but that need is non-aesthetic – the longing for an idyll, a belief in the primordial existence of the artistic, good man. The recitative was held to be the rediscovered language of those primitive men; opera was seen as the rediscovered country of that idyllically or heroically good creature, who obeyed a natural artistic impulse in all that he did, and every time he had something to say sang it at least in part, bursting fully into song at the slightest stirring of the emotions. We are not concerned to point out that with this newly created image of the paradisiacal artist the humanists of the day were doing battle with the old ecclesiastical idea of man as irredeemably corrupt and damned, so that opera can be seen both as the opposition dogma of the good man, and at the same time as an antidote to the pessimism that was such a temptation to the serious-minded people of the day, given the terrible uncertainties of every condition of life at that time. It is enough that we should recognize how the true magic, and hence the genesis of this art form, lay in the satisfaction of a thoroughly non-aesthetic need, in the optimistic glorification of man himself, in the image of primitive man as naturally good and artistic, a principle that opera gradually transformed into a menacing and terrible *demand* which, in the face of the socialist movements of the present day, we can no longer ignore. The 'noble savage' is claiming his rights. A paradisiacal prospect indeed!

I should like to add an equally clear confirmation of my view that opera is built on the same principles as our own Alexandrian culture. Opera is the offspring of theoretical man, the critical layman, not the artist: one of the most surprising facts in the history of all the arts. It was truly unmusical listeners who demanded that the words should be understood above all else; so that a rebirth of music could only occur when a way of singing was discovered in which the words would hold sway over counterpoint as a master holds sway over his servant. For the words, it was felt, were nobler than the accompanying harmonic system just as the mind is nobler than the body. It was with just this amateur, unmusical crudeness that the combinations of music, image and word were treated in the earliest days of opera; and it was in the spirit of this aesthetic that the first experiments were encouraged by the elegant amateur circles, amongst the poets and singers that they patronized. The man who is incapable of art creates for himself a kind of art by the very fact that he is the inartistic man as such. Because he has no notion of the Dionysiac depths of music, he transforms musical enjoyment into a rationalistic words-and-music rhetoric of passion in the *stilo rappresentativo*, and into a voluptuous sensuality of vocal music; because he is incapable of vision he forces the mechanic and the decorative artist into his service; because the true essence of the artist is beyond his comprehension, he conjures up the 'artistic primitive man' in accordance with his own taste, the man who passionately sings and declaims. He dreams himself into an age in which passion alone suffices to produce songs and poems: as if the emotions had ever been capable of artistic creation. Opera is based on a fallacious belief concerning the artistic process, the idyllic belief that anyone capable of emotion is an artist. According to this belief, opera is the expression of amateurism in art, dictating its laws with the cheerful optimism of theoretical man.

If we wish to combine the two ideas which we have just shown to have influenced the origin of opera within a single concept, we need only speak of an *idyllic tendency in opera*: and we need look no further than Schiller's formulation and explanation. Either, Schiller says, nature and the ideal are objects of grief, when the former is portrayed as lost and the latter as unattainable; or else both are objects of joy, being portrayed as real. The first of these is represented by the elegy in a narrow sense, the latter by the idyll in the broadest sense. Here we should immediately point out the common feature of these two ideas in the genesis of the opera – that the ideal is not felt to be unattainable, nor nature to be lost. According to this sentiment, man enjoyed a prehistoric age in which he dwelt within the very heart of nature, and thanks to his natural state he had directly accomplished the ideal of humanity, in paradisiacal virtue and artistry. And from this primitive man we are all supposed to be descended – indeed we are his very image. In order to recognize ourselves as these primitive men all we need to do is cast some things aside, voluntarily relinquishing our superfluous scholarship, our excessive culture. It was to such a consonance of nature and the ideal, to such an idyllic reality, that the cultured man of the Renaissance allowed himself to be returned by his operatic imitation of Greek tragedy, and he used that tragedy as Dante used Virgil, to reach the gates of paradise: although from that point onwards he continued the journey alone, and passed over from an imitation of the supreme Greek art form to a 'restitution of all things', an imitation of man's original art world. What good-natured confidence there was in these bold strivings, in the very midst of theoretical culture! – only to be explained by the comforting belief that 'man in himself' was the eternally virtuous operatic hero, the eternally piping or singing shepherd, who must always finally rediscover himself as such, if indeed he had ever really lost himself for any time; only to be seen as the fruit of that optimism that now rises like a sickly and seductive column of scented vapour from the depths of the Socratic world-view.

So the face of opera is not marked by the elegiac pain of eternal loss, but rather by the cheerfulness of eternal rediscovery, the cosy enjoyment of an idyllic reality, which can at least be imagined as real at any time – perhaps, at the same time, with a sense that this supposed reality is nothing but a fantastically silly dalliance, which would make anyone capable of comparing it with the terrible seriousness of nature as it really is, or with the primal scenes of mankind's actual origins, cry in disgust: 'Away with the phantom!'

Nevertheless, we would be wrong to believe that such a trifling matter as opera could simply be exorcized, like a ghost, by a vigorous shout. Anyone wishing to destroy opera must take up arms against the Alexandrian cheerfulness that uses it so naïvely as a way of expressing its favourite idea, whose true art form it is. But what could art itself expect from the effects of a genre whose origins lie outside the realm of aesthetics, which has rather crept across from a half-moral sphere to the realm of art, deceiving us only every now and again about its hybrid origins? What juices nourish this parasitic creature, opera, if not those of true art? Would we be wrong to suppose that, beneath its idyllic seductions, its Alexandrian blandishments, the supreme and properly serious task of art – that of rescuing the eye from gazing into the horrors of night and releasing the subject, with the healing balm of illusion, from the convulsive stirrings of the will – might degenerate into an empty and frivolous amusement? What becomes of the eternal truths of the Dionysiac and the Apolline in a mixture of styles such as I have shown to be the essence of *stilo rappresentativo*? Where music is considered the servant, the text the master, and where music is compared to the body, the text to the soul? Where the highest goal is at best a descriptive tone-painting, like that of the New Attic Dithyramb? Where music is utterly estranged from its true dignity as a Dionysiac mirror to the world, to the point where, a slave to appearance, it can only imitate the forms of the phenomenal world, and from the play of lines and proportions produce a superficial amusement? Close observation reveals that this fatal influence of opera on music practically coincides with the whole of the development of modern music; the optimism that lurks in the genesis of opera and in the essence of the culture it represents has managed with frightening rapidity to divest music of its Dionysiac cosmic significance, and to turn it into a formally playful entertainment; a transformation which we might only compare, say, with the metamorphosis of Aeschylean man into the cheerful man of the Alexandrians.

But if we are right, in our exemplification, to compare the disappearance of the Dionysiac spirit with a highly striking but as yet unexplained transformation and degeneration in Greek man, what hopes must awaken in us when all the most certain signs augur *the opposite process, the gradual awakening of the Dionysiac spirit, in our contemporary world*! The divine power of Heracles cannot lie eternally dormant in the prodigal service of Omphale. From the Dionysiac soil of the German spirit a power has arisen that has nothing in common with the original conditions of Socratic culture: that culture can neither explain nor excuse it, but instead finds it terrifying and inexplicable, powerful and hostile – *German music*, as we know it pre-eminently in its mighty sun-cycle from Bach to Beethoven, from Beethoven to Wagner. Even under the most favourable conditions, what can the knowledge-hungry Socratism of our own times do with this daemon rising from the bottomless depths? Neither in the flourishes and arabesques of operatic melody nor with the help of the arithmetical abacus of the fugue and contrapuntal dialectics shall we find the formula by whose thrice powerful light that daemon might be subjugated and compelled to speak. What a spectacle it is to see our aestheticians, armed with the butterfly net of their own peculiar 'beauty', beating the air as they chase after the spirit of music, while it scampers away before them with an incomprehensible life, their movements falling sadly short of any standards of eternal beauty or sublimity! Let us take a close look at these patrons of music in the flesh, as they tirelessly call 'Beauty! Beauty!' – do they really behave like nature's favourite children, formed and coddled in the lap of beauty, or are they not rather in search of a deceptive disguise for their own clumsiness, an aesthetic pretext for their own unfeeling sobriety? I am thinking of Otto Jahn, for example. But the liar and hypocrite should take care with German music, for in the whole of our culture it is the only pure, clear and cleansing fire-spirit from which and towards which, as in the teaching of the great Heraclitus of Ephesus, all things move in a double orbit. Everything that we now call culture, education and civilization will one day appear before that infallible judge, Dionysus.

Let us, then, recall how through Kant and Schopenhauer the spirit *of German philosophy*, which flows from the same sources, was able to destroy scientific Socratism's complacent delight in existence by demonstrating its limitations, and how it thus introduced an infinitely more profound and serious consideration of ethical questions and art, which we might almost describe as *Dionysiac wisdom* in conceptualized form. Whither does the mystery of the union of German music and German philosophy point, if not to a new mode of existence of which we can only gain an inkling through Greek analogies? For the Greek model is of inestimable value to us as we stand at the boundary between two different modes of existence; all transitions and struggles assume classical and instructive form in that model. Only we seem to be experiencing the great epochs of Hellenism in *reverse* order, and seem now, for example, to be moving backwards from the Alexandrian age to the tragic period. And as we do so we have a sense that the birth of a tragic age for the German spirit would mean only a return to itself, a blissful self-rediscovery. For a long time terrible external invading powers had forced it, living as it did in a helpless barbarism of form, into slavery under their own form. Now at last, having returned to the original source of its being, it can dare to stride bold and free before all peoples, freed from the apron-strings of Romance civilization; if it can only learn constantly from one nation, the Greeks – to learn from them is already in itself a glorious thing and a rare distinction. And when have we ever needed these supreme teachers more than we need them today, as we experience *the rebirth of tragedy*, and risk neither knowing whence it comes nor being able to tell whither it seeks to go?

20

One day an impartial judge may determine in which age, in which men the German spirit has most resolutely striven to learn from the Greeks; and if we confidently assume that this honour must go to the noble cultural battle of Goethe, Schiller and Winckelmann, we might at least add that since that time, since the immediate influence of that battle, the effort to find a similar path towards culture and the Greeks has incomprehensibly grown weaker and weaker. Lest we despair entirely of the German spirit, should we not conclude from this that at some important point even those warriors may have failed to penetrate to the core of Hellenism and forge a lasting alliance between German and Greek culture? – An unconscious acknowledgement of their failure may even have prompted the despondent doubt, even in serious minds, as to whether they would ever travel further along that cultural path than such illustrious predecessors had done, and whether they would ever reach their goal. This is why our own estimation of the value of the Greeks for culture has deteriorated so alarmingly since that time. The voice of compassionate condescension resounds in the most diverse encampments of the spirit and the daemon. In other camps a great deal of utterly ineffectual and vacuous rhetoric is also uttered about 'Greek harmony', 'Greek beauty' and 'Greek cheerfulness'. And those very people who might have achieved dignity by drinking indefatigably from the depths of the Greek stream, the teachers in our institutions of higher learning, have learnt most efficiently to come to terms with the Greeks, quite quickly and comfortably, often by sceptically renouncing the Hellenic ideal and utterly perverting the true intention of classical studies in all their forms. Anyone in those circles who has not expended all his energy in his efforts to become a reliable corrector of old texts, or a microscopic examiner of language, is probably trying to assimilate the Hellenic age and other ancient periods 'historically', but according to the methods and with the superior demeanour of our contemporary cultured historiography. The cultural power of our academies has never been lower or weaker than it is at present; the 'journalist', the paper-slave of the day, has emerged victorious over the academic in all cultural areas, and the academic's only resort is that metamorphosis familiar from the past, moving – if we may adopt the language of the journalist – with the 'weightless elegance' of that sphere, as a cheerful and cultured butterfly. How painfully confused the cultured men of such an era must be to behold a phenomenon that can only be grasped by comparison with the very Hellenic genius that they have never understood – the reawakening of the Dionysiac spirit and the rebirth of tragedy? In no other artistic age have so-called 'culture' and art itself been so mutually hostile as we see them today. We can understand why such a feeble culture hates true art: it fears that it will bring about its downfall. But might an entire cultural epoch, the Socratic–Alexandrian, have come to an end after tapering to the fine culminating point of contemporary culture? If such heroes as Schiller and Goethe were unable to penetrate the enchanted portal leading to the Hellenic magic mountain, if their bravest strivings brought them no further than the yearning gaze with which Goethe's Iphigenie looked from barbaric Tauris to her home across the sea, what hope remains to their successors unless that portal should open of its own accord, in a quite different place quite untouched by all previous cultural endeavours – amidst the mystic strains of reawakened tragic music?

Let no one seek to blight our faith in a future rebirth of Hellenic antiquity; for here and only here do we find our hope for a renewal and purification of the German spirit through the fire-magic of music. In the weary exhaustion of contemporary culture, what else could we name that might lead us to expect consolation from the future? We seek in vain for a single vigorously branching root, a patch of fertile and healthy soil: nowhere is there anything but dust, sand, petrification, drought. The disconsolate and isolated man could find no better symbol for this than the knight with death and the devil, as Dürer drew him for us: the armoured knight with the stern, cold gaze, who must pursue his dreadful path undaunted by his terrible companions, yet hopeless, alone with horse and hound. One such knight was our own Schopenhauer; he lacked all hope, but sought the truth. He is peerless.

But what changes come upon the weary desert of our culture, so darkly described, when it is touched by the magic of Dionysus! A storm seizes everything decrepit, rotten, broken, stunted; shrouds it in a whirling red cloud of dust and carries it into the air like a vulture. In vain confusion we seek for all that has vanished; for what we see has risen as if from beneath the earth into the gold light, so full and green, so luxuriantly alive, immeasurable and filled with yearning. Tragedy sits in sublime rapture amidst this abundance of life, suffering and delight, listening to a far-off, melancholy song which tells of the Mothers of Being, whose names are Delusion, Will, Woe.

Yes, my friends, join me in my faith in this Dionysiac life and the rebirth of tragedy. The age of Socratic man is past: crown yourselves with ivy, grasp the thyrsus and do not be amazed if tigers and panthers lie down fawning at your feet. Now dare to be tragic men, for you will be redeemed. You shall join the Dionysiac procession from India to Greece! Gird yourselves for a hard battle, but have faith in the miracles of your god!

21

To return from these hortatory notes to a mood more appropriate to contemplation, I shall repeat that only the Greeks can teach us what such a sudden and miraculous awakening of tragedy means to the innermost soul of a people. The people of the tragic mysteries was the people that fought the Persian wars, and the people that fought those wars in turn required tragedy as a restorative. Who would have imagined that this people, after it had been stirred to the very heart over several generations by the most intense paroxysms of the Dionysiac daemon, could still produce such an evenly powerful effusion of the simplest political feeling, such natural patriotic instincts and such a primal, manly delight in combat? Whenever Dionysiac excitements have reached a significant level, we may always sense how the Dionysiac release from the fetters of individuation is made tangible in a diminution, to the point of indifference or even of hostility, of political feelings; just as clearly, Apollo, the founder of states, is also the genius of the *principium individuationis*, and state and patriotism cannot live without the affirmation of the individual personality. The only path that a people can take from the orgiastic spirit is that of Indian Buddhism, which, if its yearning for the void can be borne at all, requires those rare states of ecstasy with their elevation over space, time and individuation; those states in turn call for a philosophy that teaches the overcoming of the indescribable displeasure of the intervening states by means of an idea. When a people unconditionally endorses the political impulses, it is just as necessary that it should take the path towards extreme secularization, the greatest but also the most frightening expression of which is the Roman Empire.

Placed between India and Rome, and compelled to make a seductive choice, the Greeks managed to find a third form in classical purity – certainly, they did not have long to use it themselves, but for that very reason it is immortal. For although it is an immutable truth that those whom the gods love die young, it is no less certain that they then live with the gods for ever. The noblest men of all cannot be expected to be as tough and hard-wearing as leather; staunch durability, as we find it in the nationalist impulses of the Romans, is probably not one of the necessary predicates of perfection. If we ask, then, what remedy it was that enabled the Greeks in their great era, given the extraordinary strength of their Dionysiac and political instincts, to exhaust themselves neither in ecstatic brooding nor in the consuming pursuit of worldly power and glory, but instead to attain the glorious mixture that one finds in a fine wine, which both fires the blood and turns the mind to contemplation: we must think of the tremendous power of tragedy to excite the life of a nation, to purify and to purge. We shall not sense its greatest value until it confronts us, as it did the Greeks, as the quintessence of all prophylactic remedies, the mediating force between the most intense and fatal qualities of the people.

Tragedy absorbs the highest musical ecstasies, and thus brings music to a state of true perfection. But then it places alongside it the tragic myth and the tragic hero who then, like a mighty Titan, takes the entire Dionysiac world on his back and relieves us of its burden. On the other hand it uses the same tragic myth, in the person of the tragic hero, to deliver us from our eager striving for this existence, and with an admonishing gesture points to another form of being and a higher delight, for which the struggling hero prepares himself by his destruction, not by his triumphs. Between the universality of its music and the Dionysiac receptivity of the listener, tragedy interposes a sublime symbol, myth, creating the illusion that music is merely a supreme means of representation designed to bring to life the visual world of myth. Relying on this noble deception, it can now move its limbs in a dithyrambic dance, and yield heedlessly to an orgiastic feeling of freedom in which, as music, without that deception, it could not dare to indulge. The myth shields us from the music, just as it gives the music its supreme freedom. In return, music bestows upon the tragic myth a metaphysical significance of an urgency and conviction that word and image, without that external assistance, could never hope to attain. Above all, the tragic spectator is overcome by a sure presentiment of supreme delight attained along a road of destruction and denial, so that he feels that the very depth of things is speaking perceptibly to him.

If, in the above, I have managed to provide only a tentative expression of this difficult idea, which may be immediately intelligible only to a few, I should now like to invite my friends to make a further effort and ask them to consider a single example from our common experience which may bear out my general thesis. In this example I shall not address those who use the images of the events on stage, the words and emotions of the characters, to help them to respond to the music; for music is not these people's mother tongue, and however much it may help them they still penetrate no further than the vestibule of musical perception, never reaching its inner sanctum. Some of these, like Gervinus, do not even make it to the vestibule. I must turn instead to those who are directly related to music, for whom music is their mother's womb, as it were, and who relate to the world almost exclusively through unconscious musical relations. I should like to ask these genuine musicians whether they can imagine a man who could perceive the third act of *Tristan und Isolde*, unaided by word and image, simply as a tremendous symphonic movement, without expiring at the convulsive spreading of their souls' wings? How could such a man, having laid his ear against the heart of the world will and felt the tumultuous lust for life as a thundering torrent or as a tiny, misty brook flowing into all the world's veins, fail to shatter into pieces all of a sudden? How can he bear, in the wretched bell-jar of human individuality, to hear the echo of innumerable cries of delight and woe from a 'wide space of the world's night', without inexorably fleeing to his primal home amidst the piping of the pastoral metaphysical dance? But if such a work can be perceived in its entirety without negating the existence of the individual, if such a creation can come into being without destroying its creator – where should we seek the resolution of such a contradiction?

It is at this point that the tragic myth and the tragic hero are interposed between our highest musical stimulation and the music. They are, at bottom, only a symbol of the most universal facts, of which music alone can speak directly. But if we perceived as purely Dionysiac beings, the myth would lose all its symbolic effect, it would come to an unnoticed standstill beside us, and not for a moment distract us from the reverberations of the *universalia ante rem*. But now *Apolline* power, aimed at the reconstitution of the almost fragmented individual, emerges with the healing balm of a blissful deception: we suddenly imagine we can see only Tristan, motionlessly, gloomily asking: 'The old melody; why does it awaken me?' And what before seemed a hollow sigh from the core of things, now tells us only how 'barren and empty is the sea'. And where before we breathlessly felt on the verge of extinction in the convulsive paroxysm of all our feelings, connected to this existence by a mere thread, we now see and hear only the hero, mortally wounded and yet undying, with his desperate cry: 'Yearning, yearning! To yearn in death, not to die of love!' And where, after such an excess of consuming torment, the jubilation of the horn pierced our hearts almost like the supreme torment, between us and that 'essential jubilation' the rejoicing Kurwenal now stands, turned towards the ship that bears Isolde. However powerfully this pity may affect us, in a sense it delivers us from the primal suffering of the world, just as the symbol of the myth preserves us from gazing directly on the supreme idea of the world, just as thoughts and words save us from the unbrooked effusion of the unconscious will. Through that glorious Apolline deception it seems as though the realm of sound has assumed the form of a visible world, as though it is here that Tristan's and Isolde's fate has been shaped and moulded from the most delicate and expressive material.

Thus the Apolline wrests us from the Dionysiac universality, and delights us in these individuals; to them it attaches our pity, through them it satisfies our sense of beauty, which craves great and sublime forms. It parades images of life before us and moves us to a contemplative understanding of the core of life contained within them. With the tremendous impact of image, concept, ethical teaching and sympathetic stirrings, the Apolline lifts man out of his orgiastic self-destruction, and deceives him about the universality of the Dionysiac event, deluding him into the idea that he can see only a single image of the world – Tristan and Isolde, for example – and that he will *see* it better and more profoundly *through music*. What can Apollo's healing charm not do, if it can make us believe the illusion that the Dionysiac, in the service of the Apolline, is capable of intensifying Apolline effects, as if music were essentially a vehicle for Apolline content?

In the pre-established harmony that obtains between the consummate drama and its music, the drama achieves a supreme degree of vividness that verbal drama alone cannot achieve. All the living characters on the stage are simplified before us, in the independently moving lines of the melody, into the clarity of a single curved line, and the mingling of those lines resounds to us in a series of harmonic transitions most delicately in sympathy with the moving events on stage. The relationships between things are thus made available to the senses in a way that is far from abstract, and we also realize that only through those relationships are the essence of a character and a melodic line made apparent. And while music forces us to see more and more deeply than we otherwise would, and spreads the events on the stage before us like a delicate gossamer, to our spiritualized inner vision the world on the stage is both infinitely expanded and illuminated from within. How could the verbal poet supply anything analogous, striving as he does to achieve that internal expansion and illumination of the visible stage-world indirectly, with the much more imperfect mechanism of words and concepts? Although musical tragedy makes use of the word, it can at the same time set beside it its substratum and its place of birth, and clarify the development of the word from within.

But we can say with equal assurance that this process is nothing but a glorious illusion, the very Apolline *deception* that we have just mentioned, which has the effect of relieving us of the burden of the Dionysiac surge and excess. At bottom, the relationship between music and drama is precisely the opposite of this: music is the actual idea of the world, drama a mere reflection of that idea, an isolated silhouette of it. The identity between the melodic line and the living character, between the harmony and the characters' relationships, is true in an opposite sense to that which we might have observed in our consideration of musical tragedy. However distinctly we move, enliven and illuminate that character from within, it remains mere phenomenon, without a bridge to reality itself, to the heart of the world. But music speaks from that heart; and though countless such phenomena might drift past the same music without exhausting its essence, they would remain nothing but externalized copies. The popular and entirely false opposition of soul and body does nothing, of course, to explain the difficult relationship between music and drama, and does everything to confuse it; but the unphilosophical crudeness of that opposition seems to have become a readily accepted article of faith among our aestheticians, for who knows what reasons, while they have learned nothing of the contrast between the phenomenon and the thing-in-itself and, for similarly unknown reasons, they have no wish to learn anything about them.

If our analysis has shown that the Apolline in tragedy has by means of its deception carried off a complete victory over the Dionysiac essence of music, using it for its own purposes – namely a supreme clarification of drama – we might certainly add one very important reservation: at its most significant point that Apolline deception has been broken and destroyed. The drama that spreads out before us, all its movements and characters illuminated from within by music, as though we were watching the movement of the shuttle as it weaves the fabric, has an effect as a whole that goes *beyond all Apolline artifice*. In the overall effect of tragedy the Dionysiac predominates once again; its final note could never echo from the Apolline realm. And in this process Apolline deception is revealed for what it is, a veiling of the true Dionysiac effect, which lasts for the duration of the tragedy. Such is its power that it finally forces the Apolline drama itself into a sphere where it begins to speak with Dionysiac wisdom, and where it denies itself and its Apolline clarity. Thus the difficult relationship of the Apolline and the Dionysiac in tragedy could really be symbolized by a fraternal bond between the two deities. Dionysus speaks the language of Apollo, but Apollo finally speaks the language of Dionysus, and thus is attained the supreme goal of tragedy and of art in general.[30]

22

Let the attentive friend call to mind the effect of a true musical tragedy in a pure and unadulterated way, in terms of his own experiences. I believe I have so fully described the phenomenon of this effect from both sides that he will now be able to interpret his own experiences. He will recall how, with regard to the myth passing before his eyes, he felt elevated to a kind of omniscience, as if his powers of vision were not merely superficial but could penetrate to the very depths; as if, through music, he was able to see the motions of the will, the conflict of motives, the swelling current of passions, clearly visible before him like a wealth of vividly moving lines and figures, and thus plunge into the most delicate mysteries of the unconscious. Conscious though he is of a supreme intensification of his impulses to clarity and transfiguration, he is none the less determined that this long sequence of Apolline artistic effects should *not* produce that happy lingering in will-less contemplation provoked in him by the works of the sculptor and the epic poet, the truly Apolline artists – the vindication of the individuated world through contemplation, the summit and essence of Apolline art. He beholds the transfigured world of the stage and yet denies it. He sees the tragic hero before him, in epic clarity and beauty, and yet rejoices in his destruction. He understands the dramatic events to their very depths, yet he is happy to escape into incomprehension. He feels that the hero's acts are justified, and yet is all the more uplifted when those acts destroy their originator. He trembles at the sufferings which will befall the hero, and yet they give him a higher, much more powerful pleasure. He looks more keenly, more deeply than ever, and yet wishes for blindness. How do we account for this marvellous schism within the self, this blunting of the Apolline point, if not with reference to the *Dionysiac* magic which, while appearing to raise Apolline emotions to their highest level, can still harness this exuberance of Apolline power into its own service? We can understand *the tragic myth* only as a visualization of Dionysiac wisdom by means of Apolline artifices; it takes the world of phenomena to its limits, where it denies itself and seeks to escape back to the womb of the sole true reality; and here it seems, with Isolde, to begin its metaphysical swansong:

In des Wonnemeeres
Wogendem Schwall,
In der Duft-Wellen
Tönendem Schall,
In des Weltatems
Wehendem All –
Ertrinken – versinken –
Unbewußt – höchste Lust![31]

(In the sea of rapture's
Surging roll
In the fragrant waves'
Ringing sound
In the world-breath's
Wafting space
To drown – to sink
Unconscious – supreme joy!)

Thus, through the experiences of the truly aesthetic listener, we can imagine the tragic artist himself as he creates his characters, like a prolific deity of individuation – in this sense his work can hardly be seen as an 'imitation of nature' – and the way his tremendous Dionysiac impulse then devours this whole world of phenomena, in order, behind it and through its destruction, to give a sense of a supreme artistic primal joy within the womb of the primal Oneness. Our aestheticians, of course, can tell us nothing of this return to the primal home, of the fraternal bond between the two artistic deities that exists in tragedy, or of the Apolline and Dionysiac excitement of the listener, in their tireless characterization of the hero's conflict with destiny, the victory of the moral world order or the discharging of emotions through tragedy as the essence of the tragic. Their indefatigability leads me to think that they may be utterly incapable of aesthetic stimulation, and that they listen to tragedy solely as moral beings. Never since Aristotle have we been given an account of the tragic effect from which we might infer any artistic states or aesthetic activity on the part of the listener. Now the grave events are supposed to be leading pity and terror inexorably towards the relief of discharge; now we are supposed to feel elevated and inspired by the triumph of good and noble principles, by the sacrifice of the hero in the interest of a moral view of the world. I am certain that for many people precisely this, and this alone, is the effect of tragedy, but it is equally clear that none of them, nor any of the aestheticians who interpret on their behalf, has ever experienced tragedy as a supreme *art*. That pathological discharge, Aristotle's catharsis, which philologists are uncertain whether to class among the medical or the moral phenomena, recalls a remarkable observation of Goethe's: 'Without a lively pathological interest,' he says, 'I too have never succeeded in developing any kind of tragic situation, and for that reason I have preferred to avoid them rather than seek them out. And was it not another of the merits of the ancients that they saw the supreme pathos as being merely an aesthetic game, while for us the truth of nature must also be involved in the creation of such a work?' After our own glorious experiences, we must answer that last profound question in the affirmative, having discovered to our astonishment, through musical tragedy, that the supreme pathos really can be merely an aesthetic game: hence we may believe that the primal phenomenon of the tragic can now for the first time be described with some success. Anyone who still speaks only in terms of those vicarious non-aesthetic effects, who does not feel elevated above the pathological and moral process, should despair of his aesthetic nature. We recommend instead that he take up Shakespearean interpretation after the manner of the Gervinus, and the diligent tracing of 'poetic justice', as an innocent substitute.

Thus the rebirth of tragedy also means the rebirth of the *aesthetic listener*, his place in the theatre having hitherto been occupied by a strange quid pro quo, with pretensions that are half moral and half scholarly – the 'critic'. Within his sphere, everything was artificial, and merely whitewashed with the appearance of life. In fact, the performing artist no longer knew what to do with such a listener, with all his critical gestures, and, along with the dramatist or operatic composer who inspired him, searched anxiously for the last vestiges of life in this pretentious creature, barren and incapable of enjoyment. But the audience has hitherto been made up of such 'critics': the student, the schoolboy, and even the most inoffensive female creature were unwittingly prepared by their education and by the newspapers for such a perception of works of art. In the face of such an audience, nobler spirits among the artists counted on stirring moral and religious sentiments, and the appeal to the 'moral world order' vicariously intervened where a true audience should in fact have been enraptured by the powerful magic of art. Or else the dramatist so clearly presented a more considerable or at least exciting trend from the contemporary political and social world that the listener was able to forget his critical exhaustion and yield to emotions similar to those experienced at patriotic or warlike moments, or when hearing parliamentary speeches or the condemnation of crime and vice: an estrangement of the true purposes of art, which at times almost gave rise to a cult of tendentiousness. But here something intervened that has always intervened whenever the arts become artificial: a swift degeneration of that tendentiousness, with the result that, for example, the notion of the stage as an institution for the moral education of the people, which was taken seriously in Schiller's day, is already counted among the unbelievable antiques of a dated kind of education. While the critic held sway in the theatre and the concert hall, the journalist in the schools and the press in society, art degenerated into an entertainment of the lowest kind, and aesthetic criticism became the catalyst for a vain, distracted, selfish, and, moreover, a pathetically unoriginal form of social companionability, the sense of which is conveyed by Schopenhauer's parable of the porcupines;[32] so much so that never has so much talk and so little thought been devoted to art. But is it still possible to find the company of a man capable of talking about Beethoven and Shakespeare? Let each man answer the question as he sees fit: his answer will demonstrate his understanding of 'culture', as long as he attempts to answer the question at all and has not already been struck dumb with astonishment.

On the other hand, many a person made of nobler and more delicate stuff, even if he had gradually become a critical barbarian in the manner discussed, might yet be able to speak of the unexpected and utterly unintelligible effect produced by a successful performance of *Lohengrin*. Only perhaps he had no admonishing, interpreting hand to guide him, so that the incomprehensibly different and entirely incomparable feeling that so stirred him remained isolated and, like a mysterious star, expired after a moment's gleaming. It was then that he had an inkling of what it means to be an aesthetic listener.

23

Anyone who wishes to test himself precisely to see how closely he is related to the true aesthetic spectator or to the community of Socratic-critical men need only ask himself honestly about the feeling with which he responds to *miracles* portrayed on the stage: whether his historical sense, aimed at strict psychological causality, is insulted; whether he accepts miracles, with a benevolent concession, as a phenomenon intelligible to children but remote from himself; or whether he responds in some other way. He will thus be able to tell whether he is at all capable of understanding *myth*, the concentrated image of the world which, as an abbreviation for phenomena, cannot do without miracles. But in all likelihood almost everyone, having subjected himself to a rigorous examination, will feel so undermined by the critical-historical spirit of our culture that it is only by scholarly means and mediating abstractions that the former existence of myth can be made credible. Yet without myth all culture loses its healthy and natural creative power: only a horizon surrounded by myths can unify an entire cultural movement. Myth alone rescues all the powers of imagination and the Apolline dream from their aimless wanderings. The images of myth must be the daemonic guardians, omnipresent and unnoticed, which protect the growth of the young mind, and guide man's interpretation of his life and struggles. The state itself has no unwritten laws more powerful than the mythical foundation that guarantees its connection with religion and its growth out of mythical representations. Let us now, by way of comparison, imagine abstract man, without the guidance of myth – abstract education, abstract morality, abstract justice, the abstract state; let us imagine the lawless wandering, unchecked by native myth, of the artistic imagination; let us imagine a culture without a secure and sacred primal site, condemned to exhaust every possibility and feed wretchedly on all other cultures – there we have our present age, the product of that Socratism bent on the destruction of myth. And here stands man, stripped of myth, eternally starving, in the midst of all the past ages, digging and scrabbling for roots, even if he must dig for them in the most remote antiquities. What is indicated by the great historical need of unsatisfied modern culture, clutching about for countless other cultures, with its consuming desire for knowledge, if not the loss of myth, the loss of the mythical home, the mythical womb? Let us consider whether the feverish and sinister agitation of this culture is anything other than a starving man's greedy grasping for food – and who would wish to give further nourishment to a culture such as this, unsatisfied by everything it devours, which transforms the most powerful, wholesome nourishment into 'history and criticism'?

We should also be forced to look upon our German spirit with sorrowing despair if it were already ineradicably entangled, identical with its culture, as we may observe to our horror in 'civilized' France. What was for a long time the great advantage of France and the source of its tremendous superiority, that very unity of people and culture, should now lead us to rejoice in the good fortune that our own culture, questionable as it is, still has nothing in common with the noble core of our national character. Instead, all our hopes reach out longingly towards the perception that buried beneath the twitching convulsions of our cultural life there lies a wonderful, intrinsically healthy, ancient power, which powerfully stirs itself only at certain glorious moments, before returning to its dreams of a future awakening. From this abyss there emerged the German Reformation, in whose chorale the future of German music first resounded. The Lutheran chorale is as profound, courageous and soulful, as exuberantly good and delicate, as the first luring Dionysiac call that rings out from the undergrowth at the approach of spring. And in competing echoes came the response from that solemnly high-spirited procession of Dionysiac revellers to whom we are indebted for German music – and to whom we shall be indebted for the *rebirth of German myth*!

I know that I must now take the friend who has been sympathetically following me, and lead him to a high and lonely vantage point where he will have few companions, and call out encouragingly to him that we must hold fast to our luminescent guides, the Greeks. So far, in order to purify our aesthetic awareness, we have borrowed from them the images of those two deities, each the ruler of his discrete artistic realm, a sense of whose reciprocal contact and enhancement Greek tragedy has given us. The decline of Greek tragedy seems necessarily to have been the result of a curious dissociation of the two primal artistic drives, a process that went hand in hand with a degeneration and transformation of the character of the Greek people. This compels us to reflect seriously on the necessity and closeness of the fundamental interconnections between art and people, myth and morality, tragedy and state. The decline of tragedy was also the decline of myth. Until that point the Greeks felt an involuntary need to connect all their experiences directly to their myths, understanding them solely by means of that connection. This meant that the immediate present appeared to them *sub specie aeterni* and, in a certain sense, timeless. The state and art, however, both immersed themselves in that flood of timelessness, finding a haven there from the burden and voracity of the moment. And, like a human being, a people has value only in so far as it can give its experience the stamp of eternity, for in this way it becomes desecularized, and reveals its unconscious inner conviction of the relativity of time and the true, metaphysical meaning of life. The opposite occurs when a people begins to understand itself historically and to shatter the mythical bulwarks that surround it. This generally goes hand in hand with a resolute process of secularization, a break with the unconscious metaphysics of its former existence, and all the ethical consequences which follow from that. Greek art, and Greek tragedy above all, held the destruction of myth at bay. The Greeks had to destroy tragedy, too, in order, freed from their native soil, to live uninhibited in the wilderness of thought, morality and deed. And even now that metaphysical impulse is trying to effect a form of transfiguration, albeit an attenuated one, in the Socratism of science which strives for life; but on the lower levels the same drive led only to a feverish quest that gradually lost itself in a pandemonium of myths and superstitions piled up and accumulated from all over the place. And the Greek sat in the midst of this, his heart still unsatisfied, until he learned to mask that fever with Greek cheerfulness and Greek frivolity, as a Graeculus, or to benumb himself completely with some dark oriental superstition.

Since the reawakening of Alexandrian-Roman antiquity in the fifteenth century, and after a long interlude that is barely describable, we have come close to this condition in the most striking way. At the heights we encounter the same abundant longing for knowledge, the same insatiable delight in discovery, the same terrible secularization, and along with it a rootless wandering, an avid rush to foreign tables, a frivolous deification of the present day or a stupefied renunciation of it, all *sub specie saeculi*: symptoms which hint at a similar lacking in the heart of our own culture – the destruction of myth. It seems hardly possible to graft an alien myth on to a native tree with any lasting success, without damaging the tree beyond repair. The tree may perhaps be strong and healthy enough to reject the foreign element after a terrible struggle, but it is generally consumed, becoming ailing and atrophied or exhausting itself in morbid growth. So confident are we in the pure and powerful core of the German spirit that we dare to expect that it will reject forcibly implanted foreign elements, and think it possible that the German spirit will return to itself. Some might think that this spirit must begin its struggle with the repudiation of Romance elements; they might see an outward preparation and encouragement for this in the triumphant courage, the bloody glory of the last war, but the inner necessity must still be sought in the ambition always to be worthy of our sublime predecessors on this path, Luther as well as our great artists and poets. But they should never believe that such battles can be fought without the domestic gods, without the mythic homeland, without a 'recovery' of all things German! And if the German is anxiously searching around for a guide to bring him back to his long-lost homeland, whose paths are no longer familiar – he need only listen to the blissfully enticing call of the Dionysiac bird that hovers above him and wants to show him the way.

24

Among the peculiar artistic effects of musical tragedy we stressed an Apolline *delusion* which rescues us from immediate oneness with Dionysiac music, while allowing our musical emotion to be discharged in an Apolline sphere and in an interposed, visible middle world. At the same time we thought we had observed how that discharge made the middle world of the theatrical event, the drama itself, visible and intelligible from within to a degree unattainable in any other forms of Apolline art. Where Apolline art takes wing, uplifted by the spirit of music, we encounter the supreme intensification of its powers, and must thus acknowledge the summit of both Apolline and Dionysiac artistic aims in the fraternal bond between Apollo and Dionysus.

Admittedly the Apolline image, illuminated from within by music, did not achieve the singular effect of the weaker degrees of Apolline art. It could not attain what epic poetry or animated stone could do, compelling the contemplative eye to find peaceful delight in the world of individuation, despite its higher degree of animation and clarity. We considered the drama, and our penetrating eyes entered its agitated inner world of motives – and yet we felt as though we were watching a symbol, almost imagining we could divine its deepest meaning, and wishing to draw it aside like a curtain to glimpse the primordial image that lay behind. The brightest clarity of the image was not enough for us: for it seemed to reveal as much as it concealed; and while it seemed, with its symbolic revelation, to demand that we tear the veil, that we reveal the mysteries behind it, that brightly lit clarity kept the eye in thrall and resisted further penetration.

No one who has experienced the need to look at the same time as the longing to go beyond mere looking will find it easy to imagine how clearly and definitely these two processes coexist in the contemplation of the tragic myth: while the truly aesthetic spectator will confirm that of all the singular effects of tragedy this coexistence is the most remarkable. If we can translate this phenomenon of the aesthetic spectator into an analogous process in the tragic artist, we shall come to an understanding of the genesis of the *tragic myth*. It shares with the sphere of Apolline art an utter delight in appearance and looking, and at the same time it negates that pleasure and draws even higher satisfaction from the destruction of the visible world of appearance. The content of the tragic myth at first seems to be an epic event that glorifies the struggling hero. But what is the origin of that mysterious feature whereby the hero's suffering, the most painful victories, the most agonizing oppositions of motives – in short, the exemplification of the wisdom of Silenus, or to put it in aesthetic terms, ugly and discordant elements – are repeatedly portrayed with such love and in such countless forms, precisely in the most voluptuous and youthful era of a people, unless a higher pleasure was perceived in it?

For to say that life really is so tragic does not in the least help to explain the origin of an art form, provided that art is not only an imitation of the truth of nature but a metaphysical supplement to that truth of nature, coexisting with it in order to overcome it. In as far as it belongs to art at all, the tragic myth participates fully in its metaphysical intention of transfiguration. But what does it transfigure, if it presents the world of phenomena in the image of the suffering hero? Least of all the 'reality' of this world of phenomena, because it says to us: 'Look! Take a close look! That is your life! That is the hour-hand of the clock of your existence!'

And are we to imagine that myth showed us this life in order to transfigure it for us? But if it did not, wherein lies the aesthetic pleasure with which we let those images pass before us? I am speaking of aesthetic pleasure, and know that many of these images could also produce a moral delight, taking the form of pity, for example, or moral victory. But no one seeking to deduce the effect of the tragic from moral sources alone, as has been customary in aesthetics for far too long, should believe that he has done any kind of service to art, which must insist on purity in its sphere above all else. The first challenge when it comes to explaining the tragic myth is that of seeking the pleasure peculiar to it in the purely aesthetic sphere, without intruding upon the sphere of pity, fear or moral sublimity. How can ugliness and discord, the content of the tragic myth, produce aesthetic pleasure?

At this point we must take a bold leap into a metaphysics of art, repeating our earlier assertion that existence and the world seem justified only as an aesthetic phenomenon. Accordingly, the tragic myth has to convince us that even ugliness and discord are an artistic game which the will, in the eternal abundance of its pleasure, plays with itself. But this primal and difficult phenomenon of Dionysiac art is only intelligible and can only be immediately grasped through the wonderful significance of *musical dissonance*: just as music alone, placed next to the world, can give us an idea of what we might understand by 'the justification of the world as an aesthetic phenomenon'. The pleasure produced by the tragic myth has the same origin as the pleasurable perception of dissonance in music. The Dionysiac, with its primal pleasure experienced even in pain, is the common womb of music and the tragic myth.

In referring to the musical relation of dissonance, perhaps we have made the difficult problem of the effect of tragedy considerably easier? For we now understand what it means to wish to look, in tragedy, and at the same time to long to go beyond that looking; we might characterize this condition with reference to artistically applied dissonance, by saying that we want to hear and long to go beyond hearing. The striving for infinity, the wingbeat of longing, that accompanies the supreme delight of clearly perceived reality, reminds us that both states are aspects of a Dionysiac phenomenon: over and over again it shows us the spirit that playfully builds and destroys the world of individuals as the product of a primal pleasure: similarly, dark Heraclitus compares the force that builds worlds to a child placing stones here and there, and building sandcastles and knocking them down again.

So if we wish to make a proper assessment of the Dionysiac capacity of a people, we must consider not only its music, but also its tragic myth, the second witness to that capacity. Now, given this extremely close connection between music and myth, we may suppose that the degeneracy and degradation of one will be connected with the atrophy of the other, that the weakening of the myth will express an enfeebling of the Dionysiac capacity. A glance at the evolution of the German spirit will leave us in no doubt of this. The inartistic, parasitical spirit of Socratic optimism is revealed in opera as well as in the abstract character of our own mythless existence, in an art that has sunk to the level of pure entertainment, and in a life led according to concepts. But in consolation there have been signs that the German spirit still rests and dreams, undestroyed, in wonderful health and profundity, like a slumbering knight in some inaccessible abyss: and from that abyss the Dionysiac song rises up to us, telling us that this German knight is still dreaming his ancient Dionysiac myth in blissfully serious images. Let no one imagine that the German spirit has lost its mythical home for ever, as long as it still clearly understands the voices of the birds telling it of that home. One day it will awaken, in all the morning freshness that follows a tremendous sleep. Then it will slay dragons, destroy the wicked dwarfs and awaken Brünnhilde – and Wotan's spear itself will not be able to bar its way![33]

My friends, you who believe in Dionysiac music, you also know what tragedy means to us. In it, reborn from music, we have tragic myth – and in that myth you may hope for everything and forget all that is most painful! But the most painful thing for us all is the long degradation under which the German spirit, far from house and home, lived in the service of wicked dwarves. You understand my words – as you will also, in the end, understand my hopes.

25

Music and tragic myth are to an equal extent expressions of the Dionysiac capacity of a people, and they are inseparable. Both originate in a sphere of art beyond the Apolline. Both transfigure a region in whose chords of delight dissonance as well as the terrible image of the world charmingly fade away; they both play with the sting of displeasure, trusting to their extremely powerful magical arts; both use this play to justify the existence even of the 'worst world'. Here the Dionysiac, as against the Apolline, proves to be the eternal and original artistic force, calling the whole phenomenal world into existence: in the midst of it a new transfiguring illusion is required if the animated world of individuation is to be kept alive. If we could imagine dissonance becoming man – and what else is man? – then in order to stay alive that dissonance would need a wonderful illusion, covering its own being with a veil of beauty. That is the real artistic intention of Apollo, in whose name we bring together all those innumerable illusions of the beauty of appearance, which at each moment make life worth living and urge us to experience the next moment.

From the foundation of all existence, the Dionysiac substratum of the world, no more can enter the consciousness of the human individual than can be overcome once more by that Apolline power of transfiguration, so that both of these artistic impulses are forced to unfold in strict proportion to one another, according to the law of eternal justice. Where the Dionysiac powers have risen as impetuously as we now experience them, Apollo, enveloped in a cloud, must also have descended to us; some future generation will behold his most luxuriant effects of beauty.

But anyone would intuitively sense the necessity of this effect if he had once, even while dreaming, imagined himself transposed back to life in ancient Greece: strolling beneath rows of tall Ionic columns, glancing up towards a horizon carved from pure and noble lines, beside him reflections of his transfigured form in gleaming marble, surrounded by people solemnly walking or in delicate motion, with harmonic sounds and a rhythmic gestural language – must he not, to this continuous influx of beauty, raise his hand to Apollo and exclaim: 'Happy race of Greeks! How great must Dionysus be among you, if the Delian god thinks such enchantment necessary to heal your dithyrambic madness!' – But one who was of this mind could find himself answered by an aged Athenian, glancing up at him with the sublime eye of Aeschylus: 'But consider this, too, wonderful stranger: how much did this people have to suffer to become so beautiful! But now follow me to the tragedy, and sacrifice with me in the temple of both deities!'

NOTES

1. This is the title of the First Edition of 1872, and of the virtually identical Second Edition of 1878, of which this volume is a translation. In 1886 the title was altered to '*The Birth of Tragedy. Or: Greekhood and Pessimism*', with the original title page being printed after 'Attempt at a Self-Criticism'.

2. *Wishing to learn from it the meaning of 'fear'?*: This is a reference, almost certainly, to Wagner's Siegfried in the eponymous music drama, who goes to encounter the dragon Fafner in order to learn what fear means, because the dwarf Mime, who has brought him up, has been unable to teach him that.

3. *And science itself*: Throughout *BT* Nietzsche uses *Wissenschaft*, which means science in the broadest sense, as the systematic pursuit of knowledge, and not just the natural sciences.

4. *in artibus*: in the arts.

5. *profanum vulgus*: the profane mass.

6. *What a shame . . . and unimaginable*: This is Nietzsche's attempt, not so much at self-criticism, as at redeeming *BT* by viewing it as premonitory of his later work, in its denial of morality as giving sense to existence.

7. *the discreet and hostile silence with which Christianity is treated*: That is very much a retrospective view of the work itself, in which Christianity is scarcely mentioned at all.

8. *Let us imagine . . . most unique?*: This quotation is from §18.

9. This quotation is from Act III, scene 3, of *Die Meistersinger von Nürnberg*, in which the cobbler-poet Hans Sachs explains to Walter von Stolzing that, in order to turn his dream of the previous night into art, he has to subject it to rules – which themselves would be valueless if they were not used in the service of dreams.

10. The references to Schopenhauer's *The World as Will and Representation* are to E. F. J. Payne's translation (2 vols., Dover Publications Inc., 1968).

11. *principium individuationis*: the principle of individuation. This is Schopenhauer's term for the way in which all our experience comes to us parcelled up, especially including our awareness of ourselves. It is therefore, for him, and for Nietzsche in *BT*, illusory, since reality is undifferentiated.

12. *Beethoven's 'Hymn of Joy'*: Nietzsche is referring to the setting of Schiller's 'An die Freude' in the last movement of Beethoven's Ninth Symphony.

13. *'Do you bow low . . . world?'*: A quotation from Schiller's 'Hymn', the most solemn part of the last movement of the Beethoven Symphony.

14. *to which Schiller . . . 'naïve'*: The reference is to Schiller's influential essay *On Naïve and Sentimental Poetry*, in which he draws a fundamental distinction between art which gives the impression of not being mediated by the artist's consciousness ('naïve'), and art which is evidently refracted through it ('sentimental'). The general tendency of latter-day art has been towards the sentimental, though there have been both kinds of art at most stages of its history.

15. *then we must . . . illusion*: Since Nietzsche, following Schopenhauer, sees our ordinary waking life as illusory (see note 11), it follows that when we dream we are at two removes from reality.

16. *indeed . . . contemplation*: This is an incongruous and unthinking adoption on Nietzsche's part of the Kantian and Schopenhauerian view that aesthetic experience is characterized by lack of interest, in the sense of involvement, in what we are experiencing, and thus a suspension of the will. For Kant, this marks a break from the otherwise pervasive demands of morality on us. For Schopenhauer, it means that art is 'the sabbath of the penal servitude of willing'. But the main thrust of *BT* is that in Dionysiac art we come as close as possible to identifying with the will. And he was later to castigate 'disinterested contemplation' as a castration of art, as he would have done even at this stage, had he been consistent.

17. *for it is only . . . justified*: This is the first of the two appearances in the body of *BT* of what is its cardinal tenet, which is repeated in the 'Attempt at a Self-Criticism'.

18. *Des Knaben Wunderhorn*: 'Youth's Magic Horn', a collection of German folk songs edited by Achim von Arnim and Clemens Brentano early in the nineteenth century.

19. *A. W. Schlegel*: a leading thinker and writer of the early German Romantic movement, who together with Ludwig Tieck translated a large number of Shakespeare's plays into German in editions which have classic status.

20. The quotation is from Goethe's *Faust, Part I*, lines 3980–83.

21. From Goethe's *Faust, Part I*, line 409.

22. *What was your wish . . . once more?*: This question and the rest of the paragraph sound one of the basic motifs of *BT* in the most emphatic terms.

23. *So tremendous is the power of the Apolline epic* . . .: Here Nietzsche makes as clear as possible the determining role that form plays in establishing the kind of experience that we have from works of art, and the subservience of content.

24. *These stimuli . . . ether of art*: This is the most succinct expression of Nietzsche's hostility to Euripidean drama.

25. Quotation from Goethe's *Faust, Part I*, lines 1607–11.

26. *One key . . . fanatic soul*: This paragraph is Nietzsche's most important statement on the subject.

27. An earlier version of *BT*, called *Socrates and Greek Tragedy*, ended here. And it is obvious that the rest of the book has a different tone. That does not mean that Nietzsche felt duty-bound to add a prolix pro-Wagner postscript (see Introduction).

28. *pain is . . . features of nature*: Nietzsche is obscure here; 'deluded away' is a translation of 'hinweggelogen', a past participle of a verb that seems otherwise not to exist in German.

29. From Goethe's *Faust, Part II*, lines 7437–8.

30. *Dionysus speaks . . . in general*: The final sentence of §21 is the conclusion of Nietzsche's highly convoluted dialectic, in the preceding pages, about the relationship between the Apolline and the Dionysiac in the tragic effect.

31. The quotation is the final lines of Isolde's so-called *Liebestod* in Wagner's drama, which should in fact be called her Transfiguration (*Verklärung*). They are also the final words of the whole work.

32. *Schopenhauer's parable of the porcupines*: This reference is to §396 of Schopenhauer's collection of essays, fables, etc. entitled *Parerga and Paralipomena*. The relevant passage reads: 'One cold winter's day, a number of porcupines huddled together quite closely in order through their mutual warmth to prevent themselves from being frozen. But they soon felt the effect of their quills on one another, which made them again move apart. Now when the need for warmth once more brought them together, the drawback of the quills was repeated so that they were tossed between two evils, until they had discovered the proper distance from which they could best tolerate one another.' *Parerga and Paralipomena*, trans. E. F. J. Payne, Volume 2, pp. 651–2.

33. *So if we wish . . . bar his way*: The penultimate paragraph uses imagery derived from Acts II and III of Wagner's *Siegfried*, in which Siegfried, having killed the dragon Fafner, tastes his blood and is enabled to understand the song of the Wood-bird, which tells him to beware of Mime, and leads him to the mountain top on which Brünnhilde is lying asleep, to be awoken by the fearless hero's kiss.